Dedicated to my mother
MARY EMMA YOUNG
...because it's time to acknowledge
that I did not raise myself

Also by Nancy Stone:
Whistle Up the Bay

WILLIAM B. EERDMANS
PUBLISHING COMPANY
Grand Rapids, Michigan

THE WOODEN RIVER

by

NANCY STONE

illustrated by

BETTY BEEBY

Library of Congress Cataloging in Publication Data

Stone. Nancy
The wooden river.

SUMMARY: In the 1870's a young girl and her
family spend the winter in a Saginaw Valley lumber
camp.
1. Lumber camps — Fiction. 2. Michigan — Fiction.
I. Beeby, Betty, illus. II. Title.
PZ7.S87795Wo   [Fic]   73-9677
ISBN 0-8028-4061-2

CONTENTS

Message to the Reader

By 1870, this country's most important source of lumber was Michigan, and the center of this industry was the Saginaw Valley. Millions of board feet were taken from the state to build the railroads, ships, cities and farms of the growing nation. Among the important centers for shipping this vital crop was Bay City, Michigan. Before the general availability of railroad transportation for the lumber, most logging was done in the winter so that the logs could be moved down rivers during the spring high waters. The winter life led by those who lived in the woods, the shanty boys, inkslingers, river hogs, must have been a hard life, vigorous, cold and often cruel. Tales told nowadays about these men seem to concentrate on the less attractive aspects of their activities, but I hope *The Wooden River* will show that they were also dogged, hard-working, adventurous and often self-sacrificing. Without them, the growing edge of the frontier might have stalled and died.

While *The Wooden River* is set near the Bay City of the 1870's, I have taken some liberties with the geography: Duck Tree Camp and the river near it are wholly imaginary. I have tried to picture life and activity that might be representative of those in a logging camp of

the 1870's. I have doubtless oversimplified in places, but, in general, this is the way those giant pines were harvested and shipped. I have tried to capture the excitement as well as the hardships of those days.

Mrs. Beeby and I would like to acknowledge the assistance and inspiration of a number of people. In particular, I wish to thank the anonymous writers of the WPA writers' project and of the various state agencies for the vast body of information I used in an attempt to give authenticity to Rose's environment and experiences. Also, Linda Heemstra of the Bay City Public Library and the librarians of the Kalamazoo Public Library were — as most librarians seem to be — genuinely and interestedly helpful. Jan Tackaberry Buck lovingly typed the first version and her enthusiasm is gratefully acknowledged.

Mrs. Beeby has asked me to thank, for her, John Cumming, director, and William Miller and Alex Vittands of the Clark Historical Library at Central Michigan University, and Wayne Mann, director, and Phyllis Burnham of the Western Michigan University Archives. Also, thanks to Shirley Miller, reference room librarian of the Kalamazoo Public Library.

And, of course, appreciation to our busy but ever-encouraging families.

Nancy Stone

1 Homecoming

"Flap, splash, flap, splash," went the paddles on the big side-wheeler as it pulled up to a pier on the west side of the river. Then, the noise stopped with a shudder.

"Bay City!" shouted a deckhand.

Unnecessary, Rose thought. After all, it was the end of the line.

She stood by the landward railing, holding her bright, new carpetbag, a gift from Grandma. She clutched her straw hat, too, in the light breeze that brought with it the smell of freshly cut wood in almost tonic quantities. Rose looked along the pier for her mother, and waved frantically with her hat when she caught sight of the tall figure in dark clothes.

"Mama!" she shouted, but put off calling out again when she saw her mother frown and put her fingers to her lips.

In minutes the gangway was down. Rose skipped toward her mother and the two embraced heartily.

"It's good to see you, dear," said Mrs. MacClaren and hugged Rose again.

"Oh, Mama, it's so good to get here! Where's the wagon? Can't we get going now? Out to Duck Tree Camp, I mean."

"Yes, of course, Rose, but let's get your trunk first. Now, where is it, do you know?" They looked up and down the pier, crowded with crew members and passengers.

"There it is!" said Rose suddenly. She darted toward a brown leather trunk, just being thrown from the deck. When she and her mother together had pulled it the length of the pier and out to the farm wagon standing in the road, they climbed onto the seat and Mrs. Mac-Claren swung the reins smartly against the back of the great white horse and they began to move slowly down the rutted dirt road.

The sun was shining and a yellowish, moving haze hung over the town to their right and left. Rose breathed deeply.

"Oh, Mama, what a lovely smell! It's like Grandma's bath salts."

"Hmmm. Yes, I suppose it is," was the reply and Rose wondered why her mother's lips were pressed so tightly together after she spoke.

"Don't you like the smell, Mama?"

"Oh, I like it well enough, I guess," said Mrs. Mac-Claren grudgingly. "It's just that, well, I don't like the lumber camp and . . ."

Rose interrupted. "Listen, Mama. What's that?"

A long-held, high-pitched screech, ending in an ex-

10

cited kind of tearing sound, filled the golden morning.
The noise came from the river bank, from a large,
roughly made building there.

"It's the mill, the lumber mill," said Mrs. MacClaren,
slapping again at the horse's rump with a sharp little
sound. The horse moved forward slowly and steadily,
her head down, her harness making a jumbled sound of
squeaks and jingles, mixed with the clatter of the wheels.

"I see," said Rose in a breathless little voice. The noise
had gone its length again, and ended. The tall smoke-
stacks at the mill let only a thin, straight column into
the October sky, undisturbed by wind, but around the
doors and windows of the mill eddies and swirls of the
golden dust filled the air. "Why, it's sawdust," she said
aloud, but to herself.

"Yes, and if there's anything good about living far
from town, it's not having to put up with all the sawdust in this town," her mother said.

The wagon was moving along an uncertain riverside
road now, but soon the view of the river was blocked by
tall piles of golden lumber, standing at the ends of the
piers and stacked hugely beside the mill itself.

"Such a lot of wood," said Rose conversationally. She
hoped her mother would talk to her about the lumber
and the woods and her father's job.

"Yes . . . and we're going where it all begins." There
was a hopeless tone in her voice. "But tell me about your
trip, child."

"Oh, that. Well, let's see. Grandma and Grandpa put
me on the boat in Buffalo and the Greshams took care
of me 'til Detroit and then they got off — did you know
they'd do that? — and I was afraid to go into the saloon
alone so I slept on a bench on the deck and I saw the

12

sunrise and it was like the ocean almost and . . . and I'm glad to be here! Oh, Mama," she said, hugging her mother's arm, "I have missed you so! I've been good, really, and I love Grandma and Grandpa, but I really wanted to be here with you."

Her mother smiled and, gently pulling her arm from Rose's grasp, put it around her daughter's shoulders.

"We're glad you're here, too, dear. A lumber camp is not the place for a girl — or a woman, for that matter — but when Grandma wrote that she'd have to go to England to nurse Aunt Maud . . . well, it seemed like we *couldn't* let you go that far away from us!"

The wagon reached the edge of town now and was moving through the last scraggly outskirts. It was often difficult to tell where the side of the road ended and the dusty dooryards began. Sometimes the road bent around a huge stump left standing in the right of way. The yards of the one-story, gray houses often contained stumps, too. Occasionally the flaming leaves of a maple stood above the roofs, but oftener the faraway dark, spiky line of the pine forest was the only sight of living trees.

"How much farther, Mama?"

"Oh, oh, child, don't start asking now! We've hours to go!"

The farm wagon crossed brown streams, which raced just a little with the fullness of September rains; it passed through endless stands of pine trees with here and there the leafy, brilliant fire of a maple sapling, or a small beech tree. Sometimes the aisles of the forest opened so broadly that the road disappeared and the wagon rolled almost silently across the thick carpet of needles.

13

Then the forest ended suddenly and before them stretched a barren plain with no trees, no bushes, no grasses, only charred stumps and here and there a milk-weed, or a plantain, or an aspen seedling with a few pale-yellow baby leaves ready to fall.

"Who did this?" asked Rose with distaste, half expecting her mother to say a dragon had been there, or a family of giants.

Her mother sighed. "The woodsmen did it, my dear."

Rose was silent in a kind of numbed unbelieving. The wagon seemed noisier than ever as it crossed this barren waste. A hill rolled and dipped on the other side and as the wagon rumbled toward the bottom, Mrs. MacClaren pointed to a small thicket to one side.

"There are raspberries down in some of those hollows. And huckleberries," she said.

The solemn frown on Rose's face eased and she smiled at her mother. "In this place?"

"Yes, actually in this place."

They were now in the pines again, and in the sudden coolness Rose shivered and drew her jacket around her more tightly. She leaned against her mother and drowsed, thinking of large, blue berries popping juicily between her teeth. The sun moved higher into the sky and she drifted into sleep for a little while.

Then the wagon stopped, and in the sudden silence Rose started awake and, frowning into the sun, looked around.

"Is this it?" she asked.

"Yes, this is it, Rose."

They were in a broad clearing, scattered here and there with sturdy, low buildings. Before Rose could see everything, her mother spoke again.

14

"There's your father coming now. Run to meet him, child."

Mr. MacClaren was tall, with strong and weathered features.

"Rose! My little girl!" he shouted as he lifted her bodily from the wagon and hugged her tightly.

"Papa! I'm so, so, so, so glad to see you! Oh, Papa!" She shouted too, and squeezed her eyes on tears as she hugged him back. In the silence after their greeting she heard laughter and, quickly opening her eyes, found herself looking at three men several feet away, watching the family reunion. Rose squirmed and her father set her down on the ground.

"Never mind them, Rose. They're harmless," said Mr. MacClaren.

Mrs. MacClaren spoke from the wagon, "I know, but I know how she feels. Being stared at." She whispered this last furiously. Just at that moment one of the men stepped forward.

"Take Snowball, ma'm?" He gestured toward the reins and Mrs. MacClaren handed them to him.

"Thank you, uh . . . Bunker." She barely smiled.

"Come on to your new home, Rosie!" shouted her father and led the way toward a cabin, nestled among the trunks of three or four huge pine trees, at one side of the clearing. As they walked, Rose felt too uncomfortable to look around. Grandma said no emotion except reverence should be shown in public.

They reached the door of the cabin and went in, her father ducking his head a little. Rose stopped inside the door and looked around thoroughly.

"Oh, Papa, it's so nice, so cozy, so little and precious. I love it!"

15

"Rose, you may like it, but you can hardly love it,"
said her mother sternly. Rose remembered that Mother
had been a Putnam, too.

"I do, I do! I like it, then." Her eyes were wide and
shiny as she walked slowly around the room that would
be most of her home now.

There were only two windows in the room, and
brightly colored saplings pressed from the outside. The
room was dark.

"Got to cut down a few of those saplings one of these
days," said Mr. MacClaren, as he swung Rose's trunk
in through the door.

The door was low and narrow and he ducked his head
as he entered. A small wood-burning stove stood in one
corner. Her mother was feeding it with one hand, and
trying to tie her apron with the other.

"Here, let me, Mama," said Rose, carefully hanging
her jacket on a peg by the door, and running to help
her mother.

"Thank you, Rose. I must get supper on," she said
anxiously.

"Where do I sleep?" asked Rose, looking around the
big room.

Her father pointed to a ladder in a corner and Rose
ran to the foot of it and looked up. Then, grabbing the
sides, she scrambled upstairs. Her head poked through
an opening into a large, unlighted loft. A little daylight
filtered through a louvered opening at one end. The
space was divided with two quilts, pushed back on their
ropes now. On one side she could see her own quilt
spread on the corn-husk mattress there and she knew it
was her room. Nat, her brother, would sleep in the other
space, she supposed.

16

"Where's Nat?" she called as she backed carefully down the ladder, jumping the last three rungs.

"Still on the lakes. He's due home in a day or two," said her father.

Rose began setting the table for supper, running from the corner cupboard to the table and back again.

"Oh, Mama, this is so cozy!"

"So you've said, Rose," said her mother drily.

One end of the room was filled with a massive fireplace and on either side were backless benches and two chairs. Mrs. MacClaren's sewing stand, a reminder of her New England girlhood, stood by one of the chairs. A kerosene lantern hung on a pulley over the long pine table. The table's surface was white from scrubbing, its edges rounded and velvety to the touch.

Delightedly Rose took each plate and cup from the cupboard. They were all familiar friends, friends she hadn't seen in the two years since her father had left the East to farm in Michigan. She laughed.

"They seem smaller than I remember."

"That's because you're bigger, Rosie-girl," said her father.

"I suppose so. Are we having beans, Mama?"

"Of course," answered Mrs. MacClaren. She was reaching into an oven built into one side of the fireplace. The teakettle was whistling from the little stove and Rose found the brown bread on the hearth and began cutting it. In a few minutes they were sitting at the table, eating. All of a sudden Rose felt very tired and sleepy. As she sat quietly, she thought she could still feel the thudding of the ship's engines in the bottom of her stomach. As much as she loved baked beans and brown bread, she couldn't eat.

17

"You've had a long trip, dear," said her mother gently. "Let me help you up to bed."

"Umm." She could hardly speak. And just a few minutes ago she had felt so gay, so excited. Now, she hardly knew what she was doing. Her mother was taking off her shoes, helping her undress, just as if she were a baby.

"Good night, dear."

She slept.

2 Exploring

"Ho!"

"Ho, the cabin!"

"Ho, the clearing! Wake up, we're here!"

It was barely day. Only the feeblest light came from the opening where the ladder reached up from the room below. Rose turned sleepily in her quilts. She opened her eyes and listened. Laughter and voices sounded from beyond the cabin. She crawled out of bed and tiptoed to the louvered opening at the other end of the attic. By peering between the boards that slanted across the opening, she could see out and into the clearing. A wagon was standing there, and a group of large men were gathered around it, helping a plump woman down from the seat and unloading boxes and satchels. A boy, a little younger than she, Rose judged, stood to one side, facing the cabin.

"Ho, the cabin!" he shouted again.

"Shut up, Jakie," yelled one of the men. "Ain't no call to wake up the MacClarens. Jes' move along to your own bailiwick."

Jakie started to shout again, but the man smacked the seat of his trousers and Jakie turned quickly and raised both of his fists. The man laughed and casually pushed Jakie in the face, sending him to the ground on the seat of his pants.

"Jakie, get up from there!" said the woman.

"Ma, he pushed me!"

"Get up."

The small crowd — Jakie, his mother, a man who must be his father, Rose thought, and the men — headed for a long building on the other side of the clearing. Each carried a box or a bundle, except Jakie's mother. Rose could see now that she was going to have a baby. The building they were heading for was very long, built of roughly finished logs, with a steeply pitched roof and several small windows down the side. Two doors opened into the structure, one at the end nearest Rose and the other on the side facing the clearing.

"What a huge house! I wonder how come they have such a big house and we have such a small one," she muttered to herself. She was shivering and her feet were cold. "Guess I'll get up and get warm," she thought, and ran quickly for the warmth of her quilts. She tried to dress under the covers, but got into a fierce tangle with her dress and finally had to finish while standing on the cold, bare boards of the attic floor.

When she got downstairs, her mother had just finished dressing and her hair was still in one long tail down her back.

"Did you hear, Mama?"

"Yes, that was the O'Connors. They cook for the camp. Set the table, Rose."

"Yes'm. I want to explore after breakfast. I may, mayn't I?"

"Rose, one thing you will have to learn is that this is really no place for a girl and I hope you will stay close to home. Perhaps I'll let you look around with your father, to see the camp, if you must, but there is to be no 'exploring' as you call it." She spoke very firmly, even with a hairpin between her teeth. Rose was about to argue, but just then her father came in, carrying a small pail of milk.

"O'Connors are here, Mame. Jakie's gotten to be a big boy."

"We heard."

"Be some company for Rose."

"We'll see." Rose remembered that tone and knew her father would not gain ground against it. She was silent, setting the table.

After breakfast, Mrs. MacClaren did allow Rose to accompany her father into camp. They started together across the clearing.

"What do you do here, Papa?"

"I'm what they call an inkslinger. I keep the books and manage the stores and order things. I'll probably be a scaler, too, and that means I'll have to go down to the rollways at the river and measure all the timber the boys cut."

"Can I come with you sometime?" asked Rose, puzzled by some of the words, but sensing an excitement that her life, she felt, had been lacking. She could discover the meanings of words later.

21

"Ummm. I don't think so, Rosie. Your mother — and I — want you to stay pretty close to the cabin. The shanty boys may be harmless. Mostly. But . . . well, they just aren't good company for a little girl."

Rose frowned at the "little" girl, but said nothing. The clearing they crossed was huge, jumbled with freshly built buildings, most of them long, whitish-yellow structures of roughly peeled logs, with low, peaked roofs and small, many-paned windows. The buildings were connected in series sometimes, one building leading to another by a covered passage. All of the structures were scattered at seemingly careless angles to each other and the ground was scuffed and bare. Stumps dotted the areas between buildings. The road ran in curving ridges through the camp.

The morning was clear, the sky sharply blue and white. Rose could pick out the sounds of axes and saws, the mooing of a cow, shouts of men, rattles and bangs she couldn't identify, metal on metal, and through it all the smell of smoke, pine and biscuits. The pines rose darkly around the camp, close in, leaning, watching. Here and there a flaming maple or yellow-dressed birch shone through the forest. Rose skipped to keep up with her father.

"What is a Duck Tree, Papa?"

"I guess there aren't any now, but there was probably a duck nesting in a tree around here, when the first logger came here, probably a wood duck."

"Who was he?"

"Who was who, Rosie?"

"The first logger here."

"Don' know. Some poor old-timer; had his own sawmill down on the river. I guess he used to cut and haul

22

timber from back here, but just after he set up this camp, he went busted — lost his money — and had to abandon the camp without logging his forty."

"His forty what, Papa?"

"Forty acres. That's how you buy timberland, in chunks of forty acres."

Before Rose could ask another question, they reached a rough-built shack, smaller than the other buildings, with a low, log threshold in front of the door.

"This is where you work, Papa?" asked Rose.

"This is it." He took a large iron key from his pocket and unlocked a padlock, opened the door, and motioned Rose to go in ahead of him. "Yep. This is the van." He seemed to enjoy answering Rose's questions and waited expectantly as she looked around.

"A van?" she said.

"Yes. We sell tobacco and liniment and mittens and socks. And I keep the books here."

"It's nicer than being a farmer. . . ." Rose hesitated.

"Not really, Rosie," he said, "but when crops are bad, well, it's good to be able to do something to earn money in the winter. Lots of us farmers do it." He sat down at his high desk and opened a ledger with a bang.

Just then the sound of running feet and a loud voice sounded outside the van. A breathless boy filled the doorway.

" 'Lo, Jakie," said Mr. MacClaren.

"Oh, 'lo. Didn't know you was here." He stopped and looked embarrassed, panting hard all the time.

He was younger than she was, Rose decided. He was wearing a shabby mackinaw and shoepacs, too large for him, but warm-looking. His hands were bare and red.

"This is Rose, Jakie. How's your mother and father?"

23

"Fine, I guess. Hi," he went on, turning toward Rose. "Wanna see around the camp? Road monkeys 'r' gone, but the wood butchers 'r' still over to the stable. . . ."

"Monkeys? Butchers?" said Rose excitedly, with a frown between her eyes.

"Yeah, the men that build the roads. And the carpenters. That's all that means," said Jakie with comfortable superiority.

"Can't I go, Papa?" said Rose, turning to her father.

Mr. MacClaren looked very uncomfortable. Rose knew he was thinking of her mother. She held her breath.

"Welllll," he said finally, "I guess if you stay with Jakie and come back quickly, you could take a walk around." He waved as they left the van, but no smile lightened his face and Rose was both frightened and excited by his concern. She wondered what could be causing both of her parents to fear so for her safety here.

For the next half-hour, Jakie showed Rose the camp and he also showed Rose to the camp.

"Hey!" he'd shout, "look, here's a girl! She's gonna be here this winter!" Rose remained patient and let him exhibit her.

They explored each of the raw, new buildings as they came to them. The kitchen building — "We live back here," shouted Jakie as they came to the back door — was a huge long room with one end partitioned off by stoves and enormous heavy worktables whose tops were sanded pine like that of the floor. The walls were chinked logs and the windows small and high. The ceilings were low and the whole feeling of the room for Rose was of a large, dark coziness.

Tables stretched the length of the eating area, lined

on each side by simple, split-log benches without backs. She tried to imagine the room full of loggers, but she had yet to see a shanty boy. Her mother's tight-lipped silence when the subject came up made Rose apprehensive, but her father seemed more apprehensive of her mother than of the shanty boys, and even spoke of several by name, and with affection. She shrugged and turned back to the kitchen. Mrs. O'Connor had appeared at the door of their quarters and stood smiling at Rose, her hands clasped across her swollen stomach.

"Hullo, dearie," she said, and Rose bobbed politely. "I'm so glad there'll be someone here for Jakie to take his mind off'n them shanty boys! Come around whenever you like, dearie." She nodded and went back into the small, dark room where the O'Connors lived.

"Yeah, Rose. Wait'll you see the cookies and doughnuts my pa'll bake. You'll see! He's a great cook." They went out the back door and walked toward another fresh, pine-smelling building a little way away.

". . . but *I'm* gonna be a river hog!" he announced firmly as they pushed open the door.

Now a hog, thought Rose. Such names. She'd ask later what that meant. Maybe she'd ask Nat, who should be home this evening.

They were standing in the bunkhouse. Rough wooden bunks, bare of bedding, lined either side, head toward the wall, foot toward the center aisle. Down the middle, the whole length of the bunkhouse, ran a split-log bench.

"Muzzle-loaders! I might of knowed!" There was disgust in Jakie's voice.

"What do you mean?" she looked at Jakie with an expression of annoyance. Would she ever understand anything he said without explanation?

25

"Oh, bunks like that." He gestured up and down the row. "So close together you gotta get in from the end."

Rose looked again at the beds.

"Why, so you would!" she exclaimed. "But why 'muzzle-loader'?"

Jakie looked at her with contempt. "Don't you know anything about guns? Figure it out yourself."

He jumped over the bench, ran up the long aisle and patted a round black stove that stood in the center of the bunkhouse. Rose followed him, walking slowly.

"Say," said Jakie, "let's play something in here before the shanty boys come." He stood with his hands on his hips, surveying the long, empty room. He was a few inches shorter than Rose, with curly brown hair that came over the tops of his ears. He made Rose feel motherly.

"Jakie," she said suddenly, "what's wrong with the shanty boys?"

"Wrong!? Ain't nothing wrong with 'em. Who told you?"

"My mother."

"Aw, all that bothers her is that some of 'em, well, don't use too nice language, and once in a while there's a rough un who's just out of jail."

Rose gasped.

". . . but mind, they work hard and won't bother you if you don't bother them."

Rose was not comforted. "Well, what'll we play?" she said, changing the subject.

"Well, let's see. Hide-n-seek's no good . . . let's see," he said again and paused to think.

Rose let the silence lengthen for a moment. She was

intrigued by Jakie and wanted to hear his suggestions. She guessed they'd be shouted and they were.

"Well, this is what we'll do!" he said finally, in a shout. With his hands he gestured around the room, explaining the complicated game to Rose. It was a game he'd made up himself, and Rose thought of her dolls, paper dolls, and the hoops and balls and games she had left behind at Grandma Putnam's. And here was Jakie, without a toy to his name, she supposed, inventing an elaborate play.

A play that lasted an hour or so. Rose was swept into
the excitement of Jakie's imagination. The bunks were
kind of shifting boats; back and forth they clambered,
Jakie shouting orders and Rose struggling to follow
them. Never before had she been so absorbed in a game,
here in the fresh, pine-smelling bunkhouse, with a boy
who didn't even seem to own any mittens! Rose smiled
inwardly at the thought of Jakie playing with her and
Arabella, the pink-and-white china doll she had brought
from Pennsylvania.

Finally, the small-paned windows at either end showed
a noon world beyond, the sky brilliant blue. They
paused, listening.

"Did you hear something?" asked Rose.

"Yeah. I thought I heard Ma," said Jakie.

They listened again.

"Jakie!" from nearby.

"Rooooooose!" from farther away.

" 'Bye," said Rose hurriedly as she ran through the
door without waiting for an answer.

"Shanty boys'll be in tomorrow," shouted Jakie after
her, "but we'll find something else to do!"

3 Loggers

"Where have you been, Rose?" asked her mother hastily and Rose expected trouble, remembering her father's admonition to 'come back quickly.' But Mrs. MacClaren turned away, toward the table, and continued slicing bread.

"Don't stand there," she went on. "We must get dinner on the table right way."

"Why, Mama?" asked Rose, swiftly lifting plates and cups from the shelf over the fireplace.

"Papa has to go into town to meet the boat Nat's coming on. We thought Mr. Borden would bring him, but he got here without your brother. Said he looked for him, but didn't see him. Most likely he was looking around the wrong pier — your papa doesn't think any too much of Mr. Borden — so he's going himself."

Hurriedly Mrs. MacClaren continued getting dinner. Mr. MacClaren came in, washed his hands, and sat down at the table. Rose thought he looked a little worried and wondered if the tale about Mr. Borden was a fib to make Mama feel better. Rose began to worry, too.

They ate silently until Mr. MacClaren spoke.

"Shanty boys'll get here tomorrow, most of 'em."

"Humph!" was all Rose's mother said.

"Well, Mame, it's kinda hard to do any lumbering without loggers," said her father gently. As if he's trying to teach her something, thought Rose.

"I suppose so, but do they have to be so rough and crude?"

"It's a rough, crude life they lead," said Mr. MacClaren with finality.

The conversation ended there, and Rose's thoughts went to the rough, ill-made buildings in which the shanty boys would live for the months they were working at Duck Tree Camp. She wondered what their work was like. Jakie would know and he'd be glad to tell her, she supposed.

"Mama," she said, breaking the silence, "do you know that Jakie invented a game? Invented it all by himself! Nobody told him what to do at all. Not even other boys!" She waited.

"That's good, Rose." Her mother ate silently for a moment. "I guess he doesn't have many children to play with and he has to make things up himself." She paused again. Now Mr. MacClaren waited, too, for her to speak. "I guess . . . it would be all right if you played with him now and then." She spoke firmly, and Rose and her father smiled at each other and went back to eating their dinner.

The meal was over quickly and Mr. MacClaren waved at Rose standing in the cabin door as he crossed the clearing toward the stables. Their own horse, Snowball, was stabled there, as well as the camp horses. Mr. Mac-Claren would take the wagon into town when he went for Nat.

" 'Bye, Papa!" Rose called, and turned back inside, ready to wash the dishes and scrub down the table. The afternoon went by very slowly for Rose. The sun shone outdoors and she could hear noisy activity across the clearing. There were loud shouts and hammering and the jingle of harness and rattle of heavy metal objects. Now and again she heard Jakie's voice, high and loud, among the others. She stood in the doorway of the cabin and peered through the branches of the pine that blocked her view. Her mother called her back, time and again, to the mending and cooking, which seemed, to Rose, to go on forever.

"Rose, even if there weren't socks to darn and bread to rise, I wouldn't let you go out there," said Mrs. Mac-Claren with irritation. "So, come back here where you belong."

Rose turned reluctantly back into the cabin, which was darker now than she had ever seen it. The whole afternoon was gone, the sun was behind the tall trees to the west and very little light from outdoors came into the room. Her mother finally lighted the lamp on the table.

Now, with the day almost at an end, the tiny windows brightened only by the fire light, Rose and her mother heard Mr. MacClaren drive in. The familiar jingle of harness and the stamping and snorting of Snowball told them she was satisfied to be home and within reach of dinner.

Rose and her mother waited expectantly with smiles on

31

their faces for the door to open from the autumn evening. They heard Mr. MacClaren unhitch the horse, and lead her, jingling, away. Still they waited. Nothing happened. Mrs. MacClaren went to the door and, opening it, looked out.

"He probably went to the shed with your father, to help settle Snowball." She smiled at Rose and they went about finishing the supper.

Some minutes later Mr. MacClaren walked in alone. Without a greeting, he said, "He wasn't there, Mame. I looked all over Bay City, every place." He hung his mackinaw on a hook beside Rose's jacket.

"What do you mean? Didn't he come on the ship?" Rose could see how tightly her mother had twisted the edge of her apron around her left hand.

" 'Course he did. I talked to the skipper and the mate. They both saw him leave."

Rose felt a cold prickling spread from her middle. She continued to set the table — salt, pepper, sugar, the teapot.

"But I don't understand . . . ," waited her mother.

"Well, I was awful late getting there, naturally. Even Borden was late. . . ." His voice shook now.

"Where did you look?"

"Every place, I tell you! I went to the Conroys, 'cause he has always liked Edmund. I looked around the mill, 'cause he always liked the big band saw. . . ."

"Ooooooooo . . . ," breathed Rose, in terror.

". . . but he wasn't there. Or anywhere. Mame, I . . . even looked in the saloons. And the stores," he went on hurriedly.

Mrs. MacClaren's face was white, but she stood steadily and listened to her husband.

"He'll turn up, Matthew. He probably didn't want to wait and went home with someone else for the night."

"I'll go into town tomorrow again and look," he said.

"You can't, Matthew. Tomorrow the men come and you must be here to sign them on." Both parents stood silently and looked at one another. Rose felt very lonely all of a sudden.

"I'll go, day after tomorrow, if he hasn't come by then," said Mrs. MacClaren and turned back to the neglected supper. "You'll stay here, Rose. Mrs. O'Connor will give you dinner. You'll be all right."

"Can't I come, Mama?"

"Absolutely not. The town will be full of shanty boys on their way to the pineries and it's not a fit place for a young girl."

The next day, after the dishes were washed and the floor swept, Rose muttered a few hurried words to her preoccupied mother and trotted across camp to the van. Her father was alone, sorting papers, as Rose slammed in through the door.

"Papa, I thought maybe I could help you," she began, taking off her wraps.

"What? What? Oh, Rose. Does your mother know you're here?" Mr. MacClaren went on looking at the papers. Rose knew he was not thinking of those papers, though. Or of her.

"I told her, Papa." She knew, too, that if he hadn't been thinking of Nat, he would know her answer was only half an answer.

"Can I help you, Papa? Have the shanty boys come yet?"

"What? Oh. No, no one's here yet. It's a little walk in from town. Be a while yet." He fell silent again.

"Can I help?" repeated Rose.

Before her father could answer, Jakie flung open the door and swung into the shack.

"Nat here?" he asked, gasping gustily.

"No. Papa and Mr. Borden couldn't find him. We're worried," she finished shortly.

"Oh." Jakie let out a long breath. As if he might collapse, thought Rose.

"Why don'tcha come out with me and we'll look for beech nuts?"

"I think that's a good idea, Rose," said her father, rousing himself from the pile of papers before him. "You run along. There'll be the first bunch of shanty boys coming this morning. One of 'em's sure to have heard of Nat." He smiled at his daughter.

"Well, all right, Papa. But I won't be long." She picked up her scarf, wound it around her head and her neck and buttoned her coat. She pulled on her mittens and Jakie opened the door for her.

The day was cold and dark. The slightest sprinkling of snow drifted down now and then. It was very still in the woods as Jakie and Rose set off up the road, which Jakie called a "tote road," away from the river.

They had walked only a little way when Rose exclaimed, "Look, Jakie, a little room, cut right out of the forest!"

"What?!"

Both of them stopped and Jakie looked at what Rose had found. He laughed, "A room, huh! That's a skidway, stupid!"

Rose flushed. "It looks like a room!" She walked with dignity into the square clearing just off the road. Three of the walls of the "room" were the dense growth of the forest, pines, underbrush, maple, birch. The road ran by the fourth side. The floor had been cleared of all brush, weeds, and trees; the level dirt was mixed with needles and ragged scraps of brown leaves. Rose spread her arms and revolved slowly, a little smile on her face. Jakie watched her, a puzzled expression on his face.

"It's not quite as big as a ballroom. A drawing room maybe," she stated. "Still, we could have a ball here," she continued very softly. For a moment she forgot Nat, forgot the excitements of Duck Tree Camp. The cold, grey forest faded for a while and she was back in the village hall she had known in Pennsylvania, and violins were tuning in the back of her mind.

"A *ball!* What're you talkin' about?" asked Jakie with irritation.

"A dance, dumbbell," said Rose in the same soft voice. "When the snow covers the ground it will be like dancing on a white carpet."

"When it snows you won't be doin' any dancin' here," said Jakie with a sneer. "Soon's they start cuttin', they'll be piling logs in here. That's what it's for and you're the dumbbell."

Rose stopped her gentle turning, but instead of listening to Jakie, she seemed to be listening to something farther away.

"Hush! What's that?" she said.

Jakie listened, too, for a moment. "Quick, into the trees," he said and dived for the edge of the skidway. Rose followed and in a new minutes the noises were louder and could be heard as men's voices. Rose remembered the things Jakie had told her about shanty boys. They were tramping along the tote road. Rose and Jakie waited and the crew hove into view very quickly. There

were only three of them. A broad-shouldered, heavily
bearded man and a smaller man in an ancient blue
army coat walked in front. They were followed by the
largest man Rose had ever seen, tall and so broad in the
shoulders that Rose wondered that he didn't have to
walk sideways down the broad road. He had a smooth,
golden beard and blond curls escaped from under the
black knitted cap he wore. All three men carried bulg-
ing grain sacks slung over their shoulders.

"Who are they?" whispered Rose.

"Some of the crew," said Jakie. "That little one's
Army Hughes, but I don't know the fellow he's walking
with, and the big guy, the *big guy* . . . !" and, without
finishing, Jakie crashed from their hiding place and, running so fast he became a blur, hurled himself at the
knees of the blond giant, who looked mildly startled and
stopped in his tracks.

"Francis Wilson!" shouted Jakie.

"Jakie, my boy!" rumbled the big man, flinging down
his grain sack and hoisting Jakie into the air.

Rose came out of the trees and stood quietly at one
end of the skidway, her curiosity excited by Jakie's actions.
She felt nervous and conspicuous, but she stood her
ground, waiting to be noticed.

"Where've you been, my lad?" asked Francis Wilson.

"Oh, my maw and paw and me, we went to Chicago,"
said Jakie.

"Did you now? You all at Duck Tree Camp this
winter?"

"Yup, and we brung our cow. . . ."

At this, all three men let out a cheer. "Milk in our
tea!" hollered Army.

". . . and, Francis Wilson, we got a girl in camp!"

36

4 Kidnapped

"And there is she!" Jakie pointed dramatically at Rose.

The other two men had stopped a few feet up the road and watched the reunion between Jakie and Francis Wilson. Now all four looked at Rose standing with her head down and hands behind her back. Army Hughes snorted and his companion grinned.

"I logged in a camp where they was a girl once," said the black-bearded man. "She couldn't hardly move in all them clothes, so she froze solid one day. They accidental stacked her in the rollways and when the drive commenced, she was floated clear to Saginaw 'fore she even begun to thaw."

"Yeah?!" said Jakie breathlessly.

"Yup. Even then she couldn't say nothin' and were

pretty stiff still, so it's lucky she looked the right size for a fence post, or they'da put her through the sawmill." He stopped and spat, a long arc to one side of the road. Rose felt confused. She wasn't sure, from her mother's reactions, what she had expected from these men, but somehow she didn't think it was this.

"Go on, go on," said Jakie.

"Oh, there ain't much more to the story. It was summer 'fore she could make herself known, and by that time she was rigged with wire and was helpin' hold in a herd of Guernseys south of Evanston, Illynoise."

Rose snorted.

All four men looked at her in surprise. She blushed furiously.

"You don't believe me, little miss?" asked the man.

Rose shook her head, but said nothing.

"Well, that's the way it is with truth," said the man, sadly spitting into the brush again.

"Come out and see Francis Wilson!" called Jakie to Rose.

Rose came forward. All three men quickly removed their hats and she hesitated in surprise.

"This is Francis Wilson," said Jakie, "and Army Hughes, and I don't know *him*."

"Straws is my name, and they call me Jack. Jack Straws, see?"

Jakie laughed.

"How do you do," said Rose politely and the three men murmured greetings to her.

"Best be gettin' on to camp," said Francis Wilson, putting on his cap. "Oh, what is your name, Miss?"

"Rose MacClaren," she said.

"Oh, then your pa'll be scaler, is that right?"

"Yes, I guess so."

38

"Your brother workin' at camp, too?" he asked.

"I . . . I guess so, but. . . ."

"Her brother's turned up missin'!" interrupted Jakie.

"Missin'? How do you mean?"

Between them, Jakie and Rose told all they knew, Rose forgetting her newly hatched distrust of shanty boys. She sensed their sympathy and interest, although none of them spoke for a minute. They looked at each other with frowns.

"Well, we'll get along now. See you later, children," said Francis Wilson.

Rose and Jakie waved and watched the three disappear toward camp.

"They knew somethin'," said Jakie. "I'll bet it's a man-catcher. I'll bet that's what it is."

"What's that?" asked Rose fearfully.

"Oh, sometimes a bad camp, or a bad boss, has a hard time getting all the men they need so they send out a crew of tough guys and they, well, they *kidnap* men to come and work at their camp."

"Kidnap?! You think Nat is kidnapped? We've gotta tell Papa!" shouted Rose and began to run up the road. Jakie was right behind her as she sprinted toward camp.

"Rose! Rose!" she could hear him calling after her, "they'll tell him! Francis Wilson and the others'll tell him!"

His voice faded as she lengthened her head start. There were tears in her eyes and her heart was pounding, and she didn't slow her steps, even as she crossed the camp clearing.

When Rose reached the van, she found her father standing outside the door with the three men they had met on the road. They were talking seriously together. Rose stopped and lingered near a tree stump until the men had gone toward the bunkhouse, and her father started across the clearing, pulling on his mackinaw.

"Papa! What did they say?" she asked, running after him.

"No time, child. I've got to get. . . ." He was running now too.

"Papa! Has Nat been kidnapped? Has he?"

"I'm going to find out, Rose. Now let me go," he said, shaking his daughter's hand from his arm.

Rose followed him into the cabin and watched silently while he hooked a peavy onto his belt and drew on his deerskin mittens.

"Tell your mother where I've gone," he said and continued, almost to himself, "Borden'll have to let Francis Wilson go with me." Without another word to Rose, he left the cabin. She followed him still, outside and up to the bunkhouse, where her father called, "Francis Wilson! Let's go! Let's move!"

The huge logger came out, and he and Rose's father moved quickly across the clearing in the direction of the river.

"Don't worry, little lady," called Francis Wilson, waving his hand back at Rose.

Jakie joined Rose again. The two stood looking after the men.

"Don't worry, Rose," said Jakie awkwardly, "Francis Wilson can do anything. They'll find him."

"Where's Mother?" Rose muttered and headed across to the barn. Her mother was inside, filling the cow's manger with sweet hay.

Rose started to approach her and then decided against it. She looked around for Jakie, and then heard Mrs. O'Connor's voice in the distance and saw Jakie, his jacket flapping about him, racing toward the cookhouse.

40

5 Man-catchers

Rose stood alone outside the barn. The wind drove
in a steady stream across the clearing, which was empty
of men for the moment, with only the blank eyes of
the raw buildings staring at her. The scent of fresh-cut
pine was very strong.

She looked away from the buildings and up the tote
road toward the river. Her father and Francis Wilson
had disappeared into the dimness of the trees. She could
hear the distant humming roar of the river and knew
she had to follow.

Quickly and lightly, her feet, as they pounded, sending up little billows of new-fallen snow, Rose ran up the
tote road. There were tracks in the snow and she glanced
at them now and then, but always her eyes looked cautiously through the trees, hoping she would not be seen.

Breathing hard, she reached the river bank, low here,
where the road ended. She stopped. Looking anxiously

41

up the river bank, and then downstream, she finally spotted two figures striding along the road beside the river. Without hesitating, she started after them.

Rose was a good runner, and she liked the feeling of her legs pumping and pounding on the hard white ground. As she approached her father's broad red-plaid back and the wide blue shoulders of Francis Wilson, she went very quietly, dodging in and out of the trees beside the road. She kept up with them easily. They seemed to have slowed and were talking seriously, now and then pointing across the river or into the trees.

As she trotted, now ran, now walked slowly, hesitated, then trotted again, she wondered what she would do if they crossed the river. Turn back, probably, and momentarily she hated being a girl.

They had gone more than a mile when they reached a small stream crossing the road, emptying into the river. Then she decided she wouldn't turn back, no matter what. She knew now why she was following them. She loved her brother dearly and, sitting still in the cabin, waiting for him to return, not knowing what her father was finding, watching her mother's quiet tears, would have been unbearable. She needed to go and was sure she could help.

She could barely hear the two men talking.

". . . know the path through the timber . . . ," came from Francis Wilson.

". . . not be seen . . . ," she caught from her father.

A few more muttered words, then they turned beside the small stream and headed into the woods.

The trees were far apart here, mostly birch and maple, bare now, making the woods strangely light above, weighted by heavy drifts of leaves below. Only the two men's noisy footsteps drowned out the sound of Rose's boots crunching and rustling behind them.

It didn't take long to reach their destination. Rose could see beyond them now, into a clearing that reminded her somewhat of Duck Tree Camp. The buildings were older, though, and smaller, their gable ends gray from the beat of weather.

The two men stopped. Rose shuffled quickly to a halt behind a tree, fearful that she had been heard. Neither man turned, but stood, shoulders rigid, hands clenched into fists. Rose looked beyond them to see what could have held them. Coming across the clearing before the buildings was a small group of men. One of them was as tall as Francis Wilson, his face covered with a rich, red beard. He appeared to be leading the group.

"Scram outta here! Git!" shouted the huge man, still striding across the clearing.

"Where's my boy?" shouted Mr. MacClaren in return.

"Git or we'll show you the door!" Rose could see the weapons in the hands of the group now: axes and peavies, clubs and crowbars. She bit her lips hard and clenched her fists in anguish.

Francis Wilson muttered something to Rose's father, without turning his head.

"Where is he?" repeated Mr. MacClaren.

The group was on the two men by this time.

"Ain't nobody here but who belongs. Now, out, you Duck Tree devils! Out!" The man slowly lifted the peavy he held.

The other members of the group — Rose counted five — moved slowly, ominously, around Francis Wilson and her father. Just as slowly the two backed out of reach.

Suddenly, her father called out loudly.

43

"Nat!"

Faintly, Rose heard an answer. "Pa!" It came from a weathered building not far away.

Mr. MacClaren rushed toward the ring of men, tried to shoulder and push his way through. He was thrown to the ground.

"Now, you listen here. Anybody's here wants to be here. Get that?" said the spokesman for the group heavily. "We don't want no trouble. Now *git!*" At this, the group moved closer. Francis Wilson jerked Mr. Mac-Claren upright and both moved backward quickly.

"Let's get outta this, Mr. Mac," said Francis Wilson. Then, louder, "We'll go get help and come back."

Together they swung around and ran back the way they had come. Rose ducked into the undergrowth, hoping she would not be seen. She was a little relieved when the opposing group did not follow Francis Wilson and her father. They might have seen her as they returned.

Instead, they turned around in a moment and moved to the center of their camp.

"Now what, boss?" asked one of the group.

"Into town and get Donnell! We'll need reinforcements. We'll shift him and the three that's left right away."

"Let him go, boss, let him go. Ain't nothing but trouble!"

"Do that and we're really in trouble. Can't let him go 'til next spring and we're over the border and long gone." The five moved away.

When they were out of hearing, Rose ran as silently as possible, stooping so that she couldn't be seen. She ran in the direction her father and Francis Wilson had taken. In a few minutes she was over a small rise and out of sight of camp. She wouldn't have cared now if her father had heard her. She breathed loudly and panted with little whimpers as she ran her fastest toward the river. She reached the bank finally, slipping a little on the snowy path, and turned toward Duck Tree Camp. The two men were out of sight already. "They must be running, too," she gasped aloud and continued to pound along the path, the river roaring and beating in the opposite direction. The mile seemed forever, and her aching lungs and racing heart forced her to stop now and then.

At last, she turned into the path leading to camp and saw ahead of her, walking now, the backs of her father and Francis Wilson. As they stepped into the camp, the minute their feet were in the clearing, they set up a loud shouting.

"Ho! You shanty boys! Man-catchers! Out to the clearing! Out, shanty boys!" Over and over they called, and during their shouting, men appeared steadily from the bunkhouse, the smithy, and the barn. Finally, there were forty or fifty men standing around Mr. MacClaren and Francis Wilson. One man, arriving late, shouldered his way to the front and, as he did so, the loggers made way for him with deference.

"Mr. Borden," said Rose's father, speaking to the late arrival, "my boy's been kidnapped. . . ."

"Blast it, MacClaren, you ain't got no right to call these men from their work! Got horses to be shod and peavies sharpened. . . ."

"But it wouldn't take more'n. . . ."

"No fights, MacClaren, no wars! We're here to log! Tomorrow we start cuttin' and ain't half the shanty boys I hired. . . ."

"But, *Nat!*" There was anger in her father's voice. Rose recognized it.

"Well . . . ," grumbled Borden.

"Couple hours, Mr. Borden," rumbled Francis Wilson.

"After dinner!" he shouted. "Git them horses shod!" He turned and waved his hands at the crowd. "Back now, back to work!" The men turned very slowly toward the buildings.

"Only an hour, or so," said Francis Wilson, gripping Mr. MacClaren's arm.

"In that time. . . ."

"They ain't gonna do anything, Mr. Mac. We know who they are and they can't get far. The road is full of shanty boys today, and the town, too. We got a couple hours. Best get organized, though."

Rose backed away. Francis Wilson and her father were talking together, of weapons and paths through the woods, and the strengths of various men. Not 'til after dinner, she thought. Why, Nat could be gone by then! She was angry with Mr. Borden and irritated that her father hadn't stood up to him. Turning her back on the clearing and the slowly dispersing men, she went toward her own cabin. Pausing in the door as she entered, she spoke.

"Mother," she announced, "they aren't going to get Nat 'til after dinner!"

Mrs. MacClaren turned from the stove. "What in the world are you talking about, Rose, and where have you been?"

Rose clapped her mitten over her mouth. She came all the way into the cabin and pulled the door closed behind her. She realized with a sudden, hot gasp that she hadn't stayed to tell her mother where her father had gone, where she was going, what had been found out about Nat.

As her mother came toward her, wiping her hands on her apron, Rose began. She told her mother everything, in a rushing monologue. When she finished, out of breath, Mrs. MacClaren gave her hands another emphatic wipe. She stepped to the door, reached for her shawl hanging nearby, opened the door, left quickly, headed straight for Mr. MacClaren and Francis Wilson, still standing together. Rose was right behind her.

"Matt, listen to me a minute," she spoke firmly and sharply to her husband. She told them both of the things Rose had seen and heard. Rose stood a few feet away and watched the expressions cross her father's face. He looked first puzzled, then startled, angry, fearful, and doubtful.

"No, Mame, they won't move him until dark. In an hour we'll be on our way over there with most of the camp."

"I think you should go now, Matthew."

"Ma'm, best wait and plan and do it right, with all respect," Francis Wilson said, his deep voice shy.

Just then Mr. Borden shouted from near the van.

"Got to go, Mame. It'll be all right. In an hour we'll be there and have Nat free." He and Francis Wilson left Rose and her mother standing in the clearing.

"Mother, they'll take him away!"

"No, Rose. Your father and Francis Wilson know best." She did not look at her daughter, but followed with her eyes the two men as they moved swiftly toward the diminished figure of Mr. Borden, standing arms akimbo, on the other side of the camp.

"That red-haired man, Mama, he won't wait, he

47

won't!" She tugged at her mother's arm.

"Rose . . . ," Mrs. MacClaren began.

"Mama, we could save him. You and me." Rose's face was flushed and her voice more steady.

"Rose!"

"Yes. Yes, we could! I know it, Mama!"

"It's impossible! They're grown men, rough, criminals, who have Nat."

"They're stupid, Mama, I know they are. They'll send someone to get reinforcements, and they won't expect anyone for a while and if we go right now . . . !"

"Rose . . . well . . . you're out of your head, child." But still Mrs. MacClaren stood there and Rose pressed her advantage.

"Mama, he's your . . . your child!" It wasn't fair, she knew, but hope gripped her and she thought her mother, too, seemed to have brightened.

"I guess, I guess we could go see. Yes! We will! They'll dawdle 'til it's too late." Without another glance around, Mrs. MacClaren turned toward the stable.

"Come, Rose, help me hitch up Snowball. Quick now!"

6 Rescue

"Come on, Snowball. Faster, faster, you old lady!"
Rose's mother muttered to the horse. Rose was pretty
sure Snowball would just go along at her regular pace,
and she was right. Steadily, at a moderate speed, the
wagon moved down the tote road. It had stopped snowing and the tracks Rose, her father, and Francis Wilson
had made just a short time before remained, marring
the white smoothness. The snow was not heavy enough
to quiet the sounds of the wagon, and Mrs. MacClaren
and Rose looked over their shoulders from time to time,
afraid of being followed.

Shortly they reached the river and silently Rose
pointed the way. Snowball picked up a little speed in
the mile they traveled to the little stream, but still it
seemed to Rose as if the horse took forever. The wind
was blowing now, and Rose shivered now and then and
her mother pulled her shawl closer about her shoulders.

"We should have stopped for a bonnet for you, Mama."

"I'm all right, Rose. Now, which way?"

They stopped at the side of the little stream and Rose indicated the path through the trees.

"We'll leave Snowball here," said Mrs. MacClaren. She and Rose slid down from the wagon. The wagon was turned around on the road and Snowball loosely tethered to a tree.

Then Mrs. MacClaren rummaged a few minutes among the things in the back of the wagon and at last pulled out a short, dusty horse whip.

"Oh, Mama! Good for you!" breathed Rose.

"Rose, I want you to follow me, keep as quiet as possible and if there's trouble, stay out of it."

"No," said Rose smoothly.

Her mother snorted, but said nothing more.

Grimly they started in through the trees. Snowball stamped and whinnied behind them.

Rose could barely keep up with her mother, as they wound their way through the hardwoods, scuffing the snow-mixed piles of leaves. Over the small rise of ground they went, and from the top they could see down into the clearing of the old camp. It lay very quiet in the gray light of the dull day. From one of the buildings chimney smoke rose in an eastward stream, blown by the wind.

"Hmmm," murmured Mrs. MacClaren. Keeping them both behind a small clump of birch, she looked for several minutes at the camp below.

"Come along. But, Rose, you must run back here if there is trouble. You must!" Mrs. MacClaren didn't wait for an answer this time, and Rose followed, looking determined. Nothing could make her turn back. This was her adventure, her idea.

Very quietly, Mrs. MacClaren, followed by Rose, trotted across the clearing to the rear of the building from which the smoke was coming. She looked cautiously through a corner of the small window at the end of the building. Rose, standing at the other side of the window, heard very clearly a man's voice.

"Give up, kid!" the voice said loudly. "Relax. Come spring you kin go back to wherever you come from, with maybe forty-fifty bucks in your jeans."

There was silence again. Rose very, very carefully raised herself on tiptoe and peered through the bottom of the window, beside her mother. The window was very dirty, rain-spotted and caked on the outside, draped with gray cobwebs on the inside.

The voice spoke again and Rose could hear it so clearly she knew the speaker must be right below the window through which they were looking.

"Just take it easy."

The chinking had fallen out of the log siding in many places. Suddenly, Rose and her mother realized that they were hearing the voice right through the cracks in the wall; they looked at each other in horror. In a moment, Rose's mother, moving very slowly and cautiously, backed away from the window and motioned Rose to follow. In a few minutes they were away from the building and again at the edge of the woods.

"That was Nat, Rose. I saw him."

"That man talking? But it didn't sound anything like *Nat.*"

"No, no. That was the man who's keeping him prisoner. Nat was sitting on the deacon seat, down near the

51

door. There was another man there, too. Sitting in front of the door."

"Are we going to rescue him, Mama?"

"Well. . . ."

"Mama!"

"Well, yes, then. There's no other way. There're only two men now, your father's too far away and we've got to do it now." A look of fierceness crossed Mrs. Mac-Claren's face, one Rose had never seen there before.

Without another word they walked back through the yard and up to the front entrance. Instead of a wooden door, there was a heavy piece of canvas across the opening, secured only at the top. Mrs. MacClaren pulled aside an edge of the canvas and Rose, pushing from behind, could see inside the dim building. Almost opposite her sat her beloved brother Nat. He was taller than she remembered and looked older. His clothes were dirty and torn and he was barefooted. He was whittling now.

Nat's eyes strayed to the man sitting at the door and then caught sight of his mother. He jumped to his feet and dropped the piece of wood he was holding.

"Mother!" he cried.

"Whaaaat?!" shouted the man by the door, whirling around.

Nat, no longer startled, leaped on the man's back, knocking him to the floor and part way out the door. The man grunted and Mrs. MacClaren shouted, "Watch out, Nat! The other one!"

The man at the end of the room had come running as soon as Nat jumped on his buddy. Nat, having trouble holding down the first man, who weighed at least a hundred pounds more than he, could not turn at his mother's call.

Mrs. MacClaren drew out the buggy whip and flailed at the second man, who retreated before the stinging blows.

Rose, in the partly drawn canvas door, saw her brother's problem and a second after the man had dropped through the doorway, said, "Hello, Nat," and calmly sat down on the man's head, where she put her feet together demurely and smoothed her skirts. She was elated and excitement filled her.

"Stop, lady, stop!" shouted the other man, who had retreated before Mrs. MacClaren's attack to a far corner of the room. By this time, Nat had twisted his man's arm to the back and was managing to hold it there as he sat on the man's legs.

"Stay where you are, then," said Mrs. MacClaren with great force.

"Yes'm," he said, cowering with his hands before his face.

Mrs. MacClaren backed toward the door.

"Nat, when I get to the door, get set to run through the clearing and up the rise toward the river. Snowball's along the way. Rose and I will follow as fast as we can." All the time she was backing slowly, and by the time she finished she had reached the door.

Nat gave a last twist to his victim's arm and, jumping up, ran ahead of his mother out through the door. Mrs. MacClaren laid a sharp blow across the legs of the man Nat had been sitting on and then turned and ran through the door herself.

"Come along, Rose," she shouted over her shoulder.

Rose gave a small bounce on the man's head and jumped up to follow her.

In a moment they had caught up with Nat and were running with him through the woods. They had reached the top of the rise before the two men came bursting through the doorway and after them.

"Keep going, keep going!" shouted Nat.

One of the men had almost caught up with them, when Mrs. MacClaren turned with her whip and prepared again to do battle.

"All right, lady, all right!" cried the man, and stopped where he was, his hands covering his head, prepared for the lash of the whip. Mrs. MacClaren simply turned and ran after her children again.

In a few minutes they had reached Snowball. Rose jumped up to the seat, Nat climbed in the back, and Mrs. MacClaren sat down beside Rose and cracked the whip she held above Snowball's head.

The poor horse was so startled by the sound that she broke into a run, something she hadn't done since she'd been a foal. Jerking the wagon around stumps and piles of brush, she plunged on along the river road. The snow had begun again, and the drifts of leaves were lost in whiteness now. Mrs. MacClaren pulled on the reins as they went on. Snowball slowed to her usual steady pace. The horse whinnied once and continued as if nothing had happened.

"You must be cold," said Rose solicitously to her brother, who not only was shoeless, but was wearing only a thin, torn shirt and trousers.

"Yes, I am," answered Nat, and pulled some of the sacks in the back of the wagon around his feet. Rose unwrapped her muffler and draped it carefully over his neck and shoulders and then, taking off her coat, put that around him, too.

"You can't do that, Rosie. You'll freeze," he said, his own teeth chattering.

54

"Oh, yes, it's all right. We'll be home in a little while and I have a heavy sweater on." She smiled back at Nat and her mother smiled warmly at them both.

*   *   *   *

When they reached Duck Tree Camp, the clearing was full of men, milling and jostling each other. Mr. MacClaren, standing on a wooden box, was talking excitedly to the group. As the wagon rattled into the clearing, he stopped for a second and the whole group looked toward it.

"We're here, Matt!" shouted Mrs. MacClaren, and Rose, still excited herself, thought nothing of such unladylike behavior.

"We rescued him too, Papa!" she shouted herself.

At that moment Nat, too, stood up in the back of the wagon and called, waving one of the sacks, "Pa! Pa! Here I am! I'm back!"

Mr. MacClaren jumped from the box, raced through the crowd and threw his arms around Nat as the boy jumped from the wagon.

"Where have you been? Tell me, what's this all about?" Rose's father asked, and waved his hand at the wagon, Mrs. MacClaren, and Rose.

"Where was you, boy?" asked Francis Wilson, coming up.

"Let him get inside, Matthew," said Mrs. MacClaren, "he has no coat on."

She handed the horse's reins to one of the men standing nearby, who took them, helped Mrs. MacClaren and Rose from the wagon, and led the horse toward the barn.

Mr. MacClaren raised his arms high and called in a loud voice, "Thanks boys, thanks a heap, but Nat's back!"

55

The group sent up a cheer, a few caps were tossed into the air, full of snow now, and the men drifted away here and there through the camp.

Rose followed her father and mother and Nat into their cabin. The next few minutes they spent wrapping Nat in quilts and rugs, bringing him hot tea and bread and butter. They settled him before the fire, and when he had finished eating, he told them his story.

"I got off the ship all right, a few hours early, too, so there wasn't anyone there to meet me. I didn't expect you, 'course, so I thought I'd go up to Conroys and see Edmund a bit. The town was really lively, with shanty boys everywhere, the saloons bursting at the seams." He glanced at his mother and blushed, but she was busy rubbing his feet with a linen towel. "And so I went there by the back streets and when I turned one corner, this big fella with a red beard. . . ."

"Oh! the one the first time, Papa . . . ," said Rose excitedly, and stopped.

"Go on, Nat," said Mrs. MacClaren.

". . . grabbed me by the arm and pulled me into a woodshed." Mr. MacClaren growled at this, but Nat went on.

"He asked me if I was looking for a job and I told him, no, I had one, but he still didn't let go. I tried to pull away, but another man came in just then, and he grabbed me, too. Before I knew what they were doing, I was tied and in the back of a wagon." All of his family gave exclamations of shock and Nat looked gratified.

"Well, they drove out of town fast and before I could get loose — it was quite a good ways, really — they'd stopped and dragged me outta the wagon and into that bunkhouse, where you and Rose found me, Ma. Well, there was four or five other fellas there, tied up, just like me, but. . . ."

"Where were they, Nat?" asked Rose. "They weren't there when Mama and I came."

"No, just wait a minute and I'll tell you. Just after I heard Pa call, not long at all, three of the men came in and tied the other fellers together and untied their feet and led 'em off. I heard the one with the red beard say they had a special place for me and in a while they'd take me there."

"Who were the others, son?"

"I don't know, Pa. I didn't know any of them. Just ordinary shanty boys. One said he was a farmer, another that he sailed in the summer and logged in the winter."

"Anyway. . . ."

"Yes, anyway, they'd only been gone a few minutes when you arrived, Ma, you and Rose." He laughed. Rose joined in, remembering the looks on the faces of Nat's captors.

"What about the man-catchers?"

"There was the big one I told you about, the one who stopped me, and two others, the ones who were there when Ma and Rose came. They looked just like loggers, with beards and dirty mackinaws and things. There were others, I'm sure, but I only heard them, never saw them. The big one left, and I never saw him again."

"Any notion at all of who they were working for?"

Nat shook his head and pulled the quilt more tightly around his shoulders. "Nope. They always just said 'the boss.' Could have been anybody."

Rose wrinkled her forehead, trying to remember something.

"Why didn't you tell them who you were?" Rose

asked, and the other three turned toward her.

"Oh," said Nat, "just because, I guess. What good would it do and they might've figured on coming here and taking someone else."

"And they took your shoes and coat so you wouldn't think of escaping," stated Rose.

"That's right, Rosie."

"Now," said Mrs. MacClaren, taking Nat's cup and plate to the table, "Nat should have a rest. Sleep in our bed, by the fire, son, this afternoon. Rose and I'll be over at the cookhouse, helping Marian O'Connor."

When Nat was in bed, quilts tucked around his shoulders, Rose and her mother and father prepared to leave. It was very quiet in the cabin.

Just to reassure herself, Rose said aloud, "Nat's home!"

As she spoke, her parents turned slowly and looked at her. She felt herself flush and a little cloud of apprehension grew in her mind.

"And I helped save him," she added quickly.

"Rose," said her father, "there are a few things I want to talk about. . . ."

And he did talk about a few things with Rose. Rose cried a little and her father was sorry and her mother defended her a little. All three decided, while Nat slept quietly, that Rose had been wrong to follow her father and Francis Wilson and that both she and her mother had been . . . hasty . . . to attempt Nat's rescue alone.

"But we did it, Papa, we. . . ."

"That's beside the point, Rose."

"But Matt . . . well, I guess we both were rash," said Rose's mother. "Now, what will we do in the future?"

"Perhaps Rose should have less freedom, Mame. What do you think?"

Rose waited breathlessly, an unfallen tear drying in her eye.

Mrs. MacClaren frowned. "I didn't think I'd given her any undue freedom, Matt." She paused and twisted her mouth, thinking. "I think it's that, well, she didn't think she could come to me, or you. Until the last possible, desperate moment." She stopped again. "I think we should leave it as it is. This was an unusual situation, after all."

"Perhaps you're right, Mame."

"Can we count on your trustworthiness?" asked Mrs. MacClaren, turning to Rose.

"Oh, of course, Mama!" It had been such a successful adventure that Rose felt full of power — virtuous and comfortable. The world was hers, no need to be anything but trustworthy. She knew her way around in the woods now, and it wasn't so frightening at all. She looked her mother and her father in the eye and meant what she said.

The next morning she sat at the table with Nat, who was eating a very late breakfast.

"Are you going to try to catch the man-catchers?" she asked.

"Nope. Gotta go to work." Nat sprinkled brown sugar on his oatmeal.

"But they shouldn't get away with that!" said Rose indignantly.

"Weeeeeel, maybe sometime I'll see 'em again, and then I'll get 'em." Milk covered the oatmeal next.

"Rose, that's enough. Let Nat eat," interrupted Mrs. MacClaren, who was sewing by the fireplace.

There was silence for a minute. Rose sat quietly, Nat ate lustily. Rose spoke again. "Only a little while 'til Thanksgiving, Nat. And then Christmas! Aren't you glad?" she asked.

"Sure. But mostly I want to get to work." He scraped up the last of his oatmeal and let his spoon rattle to rest in the bowl.

60

"Where are you going to work?" Rose looked wistfully at her tall, gangly brother.

"Well, I guess I'm s'posed to work over to the cookhouse. . . ."

"*At* the cookhouse," interposed his mother.

"At the cookhouse, then. But, I'd really like to work in the woods." He half turned toward his mother as he said this. "I'm big enough to be a swamper, or something." Rose caught the edge of rebellious frustration in his voice.

"Nat, we've been all over that! A logging crew is no place for a fourteen-year-old boy. Now I don't want to hear any more about it." Mrs. MacClaren turned to her sewing with a flourish.

Nat muttered under his breath. Only Rose heard him and she said nothing.

He spoke up again. "Maybe in the spring, Ma? Maybe I could be a river hog." His eyes lighted.

"Nathan!" said his mother warningly.

"What's a river hog?" Rose asked. Her mother went back to her sewing.

"It's a man who helps guide the logs down the river during the spring drive." Now his sad face looked wistful as well.

"Is it exciting?" asked Rose.

"That's enough, Rose," said her mother. "Come and help with these hems."

So in a day or two Nat went to the cookhouse and began to help Jake, who was Jakie's father and the camp cook. Nat worked hard for his little money, wages that his father saved for him. Whenever he could, he talked to the shanty boys; and Rose, seeing him listening breathlessly to Francis Wilson, or Army, or Stove McCoy, wished desperately that she was free to join the conversation.

"It'll be cold out there tonight!" exclaimed Mr. MacClaren when he came in for supper one evening. "Yep, should be just right for icing tonight."

"Oh, Matthew, must you?" said Mrs. MacClaren anxiously.

Rose waited, still setting the table quietly, to hear why her mother was disturbed.

"I must, Mame, it's part of my job. I'll take Junction and Nat."

"Nat! But he's just a boy!" said Rose's mother.

"He'll be all right. We all will," said Mr. MacClaren impatiently.

"But it's such hard work. And in this cold and wind! And you might slide off the road and overturn."

"Hard work and cold won't hurt us and we *could* be hit by a thunderbolt, but we won't." Rose knew, from the way her father said this, that there would be no more discussion.

After Nat's supper in the cookhouse, he came home to put on extra sweaters and socks. Rose sensed his excitement.

"Oh, Papa, can't I come too?"

"No, 'course not! You're a girl," said Nat.

"I asked Papa!" snapped Rose.

"Nat's right, Rose," said Mr. MacClaren. He turned to his wife. "But let Rose come to the road in about an hour and a half with a bucket of hot coffee," he said. Rose looked hopefully at her mother.

"All right, all right," her mother said, after a moment.

After Nat and her father had gone, Rose cleared and washed the dishes, doing it very carefully and very slowly, so that the task would take up the whole time until she left. Finally, after she finished sweeping the hearth her mother said, "It's time you were starting, Rose. Put a scarf over your face, please." She handed Rose the dark-blue coffeepot and three tin mugs. "Just go wait by the road, but not too close," she said, tugging Rose's cap down.

Rose left the cabin and walked across the clearing. The paths were easy to see in the brilliant light of the three-quarter moon. The wind was still now and Rose could hear very clearly many sounds in the night. As she walked by the bunkhouse, she could hear the small wail of a mouth organ. The two pigs in their pen under the cookhouse porch grunted and whistled occasionally.

She put the coffeepot down on a stump and waited beside the road. She could hear rattling and clanking up the road, and in a few minutes two horses hove into sight, pulling a sleigh. The driver halted the horses and he and two other figures on the sleigh jumped down and came to where Rose stood.

"Good to see you, Miss," said Junction, taking the cup of hot coffee Rose handed him. Nat and Mr. Mac-Claren murmured their thanks, too, through the steam that rose from their cups.

Rose wandered over toward the sleigh and stood looking at it. The runners of iron were huge, a giant's sled, Rose thought. Stretched across the back of the sleigh was a long wooden box.

"Look like someone's coffin?" Nat had come up behind Rose and grinned as he asked the question.

"Yes!" said Rose, shivering. "But what are all the holes?"

"That's where the water comes out, but it's empty

63

now. In fact," he said, leaping to the back of the sleigh
where several large barrels stood behind the "coffin,"
"I've got to fill it now."

He pushed the hose into the top of one barrel and,
sucking briefly on the other end, started the water running into a hole in the top of the watering box. As soon
as the water started flowing, he jumped down and,
quickly taking a fistful of corks from his pocket, plugged
up the holes as fast as he could! Rose could see that it
was a kind of game with him. She awaited its outcome.

"There! Did it!" he shouted triumphantly. "Got 'em all in before the water started coming out.

"Why don't you put them in first?" asked Rose.

"More fun this way," said Nat, putting on his mittens.

The horses stamped uneasily, the steam rising from their nostrils in the pale light.

"Let's get on with it, Junction," said Mr. MacClaren, " 'bout filled again, Nat?"

"Will be in a second," said Nat, moving his siphon hose to another barrel.

In a few minutes Junction had thrown the empty barrels off the sleigh and Mr. MacClaren had slapped the reigns and started the horses moving.

Rose watched Nat, lying on his stomach on the watering box, pulling out corks almost as fast as he had put them in. Even from a distance she could see that he had taken off his mittens again and his fingers were red and stiff. When all the corks were out, streams of water shone silver in the moonlight, glistening a moment where they hit the road and then slowly losing their shine as the water froze.

The harness jangled and the sleigh squeaked as it moved away from camp. Rose took one short slide on the icy road and ran back to the stump for the coffeepot and cups and then hurried home.

TIM-M-BER!

Rose ate the last of her Indian pudding.

"Well," she said with satisfaction, "that's gone. I thought it would last forever."

Her father laughed. "If you hadn't made such a lot for Thanksgiving it would have been gone before this."

"I thought you liked it, Rose," said her mother.

"I do," said Rose, getting up to stack the dishes, "but not for the rest of my life."

Her parents laughed and rose from the table also.

"Well, they started pulling 'em to the rollways this morning, and in a few days there'll be enough stacked at the river, so I'll be out there most of the day," said her father, pulling on his shoepacs.

"Tsk, dear," said Mrs. MacClaren, "it seems as if you do more than anyone around here."

"That's not true, Mame, I just do my job." He finished putting on his mittens, jacket, and knitted cap and

67

opened the door. A swirl of snow came in before he could say good-bye and close it behind him.

"What does he mean, Mama?"

"He means that he doesn't think Mr. Borden overworks him," Mrs. MacClaren answered.

"No, no, mother! I mean about the rollways and that," said Rose.

"Oh. Well, it needn't concern us. It just means they've hauled logs from where they were cut to the skidways along the tote road."

Rose nodded and went on with her work. After she had done the dishes, her mother gave her some drill in arithmetic and spelling and then Rose took up her knitting. Her thoughts drifted here and there. Christmas would be next; then spring; then the log drive. Her mother had said something about a trip to town! She wondered what the shanty boys were doing. She thought about Nat's kidnappers and wondered where they were. No one seemed to be worrying about finding out who they were, catching them, punishing them. She wondered if the old camp was being used this winter.

Just then, Jakie's voice was heard calling outside the cabin.

"Rooooose! Ro-o-o-o-se!" Rose's needles stopped clicking and she looked hopefully at her mother. When Mrs. MacClaren didn't look up, Rose ventured to clear her throat and say softly, "Please, Mama?"

"Well, all right. I guess you haven't had much fresh air lately. . . ."

Before she had finished, Rose had bundled up her knitting and was into her jacket. "Back at supper time, Mama!" she called.

68

"What'll we do?" asked Jakie, when Rose had joined him.

"I don't care," said Rose. Her face was cold, but the sting felt good.

The two scuffed along the path that had been shoveled through the snow toward the barn. The day was cold and windy, although the snow had stopped now. For a while they stood in front of the blacksmith shop. There the snow had become a sloppy brown stew, squishing over the insteps of Rose's rubber boots.

"Jakie, want to know a secret?" asked Rose finally.

"What? Girls' secrets aren't much!"

"I'm going to where Nat was kidnapped to." She ignored his last remark.

"What!"

"Yes. Hush, don't shout, don't tell anyone," she whispered as old Blackie looked up from a horseshoe. "Let's go over here," she said, pulling him over toward a corner of the barn.

"Want to come?" she asked.

"Well, I guess so. Where is it?"

"I know, about. Through the woods, that way. We daren't go by the river. Papa might be there. I'm not sure he'd want me to go."

"I know he wouldn't," said Jakie.

"But I think the kidnappers will come back. I want to spy on them," said Rose importantly.

"Oh, come on," said Jakie soothingly. "Let's stay here, instead. Maybe Pa'll let us play train in the cookhouse."

"No. Let's go into the woods. Maybe we'll see some shanty boys working," she said alluringly.

"Well, well! Francis Wilson is cutting over in that direction, too."

69

"Let's go then. Nothing can possibly happen. We'll be back by dinner time."

"Well, I don't think we ought to . . . ," said Jakie, but Rose was pulling his sleeve.

"You know the way, Jakie. You lead."

He began to move. In a few minutes they were in the forest. The walking was not easy through the trees. In its whiteness the snow hid fallen branches, holes, roots. Rose stumbled constantly. Jakie kept encouraging her and helping her over the worst spots. She began to wish she had never come.

"Let's go back," she said, panting, just after falling into a pile of sodden leaves.

"Listen! There they are now. We *can't* go back. This was your idea. We'll watch Francis Wilson a while and then go on to the old camp. You want to catch those kidnappers, don't you?"

He spoke with urgency, so Rose picked herself up and followed him through the trees.

"Stop here," Jakie whispered after a few minutes. Rose looked out through the remaining trees toward the sound of the ringing axes. She gave a small gasp.

The forest all but ended here. In front of them, Francis Wilson and Jack Straws were swinging bright axes at the trunk of a huge pine. Beyond them was a cluster of stumps, almost hidden in a big pile of branches, still laden with pine needles. Past the stumps Rose could see nothing but black-dotted snow for acres and acres, it seemed. Toward the horizon the leafless lines of a stand of maples cut the sky.

"Where are all the trees?" she whispered. Jakie looked at her with his mouth open.

"Where do you think? They've cut them down and

70

they're out in the skidways, or on their way to the river."
He continued to look at her in amazement.

"They're cutting them *all* down?"

"If they can," answered Jakie matter-of-factly, and
turned to watch the two fallers. They worked rhyth-
mically and not too fast.

To Rose their motions seemed strong and almost
beautiful. Her eyes followed the soaring pine on which
they worked as it pierced the leaden sky.

"Won't it fall on them?"

"No, stupid, they know exactly where it will fall,"
answered Jakie.

Just then a voice sounded to one side. "Come on,
come on, get it down!" It was Army Hughes, coming up
the skidroad, leading a horse.

"What does he do?" asked Rose in a low voice.

"He's a swamper," said Jakie. "He clears the road
out to the tote road, he cuts the limbs and branches off
the tree once it's down, and he helps hitch up the tree
and pull it out to the skidway after that."

"But the road's already cleared."

"Now, yes, but this'll probably be the last tree they'll
take from here. From here to camp it's too mixed with
hardwoods — maples and stuff, you know. Anyway, when
they move some place else, he'll have to clear a road."

The swamper spoke again. "Come on, it's almost dinner time and this blankety wind'll be the end of me."

"Stop your mouth, Army," said Jack in between
strokes.

"Let's go around on the other side. We can see better," said Jakie. Before Rose could answer, the boy was
creeping, bent over, through the trees to their right
and around toward the cluster of stumps on the other

71

side. Rose followed him apprehensively. In a few minutes they were crouched down behind two stumps, the pile of branches in front of them. It had started to snow again and the flakes got in Rose's eyes as she tried to watch the men.

Soon the men stopped chopping and Jack picked up two wedges of wood and with the back of his axe pounded them into the deep cut they had made. Both the fallers put down their axes and picked up a long two-man saw. They began to saw the trunk on the side away from the wedges.

"Why don't they use the saw all the time?" asked Rose.

"Oh, they're still old-fashioned, my pa says. There'll come a day when they'll use the saw on both sides," whispered Jakie.

Shortly Rose heard a kind of splintery crack. Jack said, "Now, boy," quietly. Francis Wilson neatly slipped the handle off his end of the saw, Jack pulled it through the cut quickly, there was another, louder, cracking and *"Tim-m-ber!"* shouted Jack. The top of the tree swayed and flopped, and very slowly, it seemed, the huge, straight trunk arched downward toward the earth. It was in that moment that Rose thought suddenly, *"They* may know where it's falling, but *we* don't!"

She stood up and screamed.

At that moment, the tree in its fall came level with her, several feet to her left. The soft green end of a branch hit her across the chest and she fell backwards. She screamed again. In a few seconds she realized she wasn't hurt, but by that time Jakie was bending over her, shouting her name, and, crashing through the woods toward her, as she sat up, were the three men.

72

"What in all git-out is happening?" yelled Army.

"You all right, girl?" asked Francis Wilson as he helped her to her feet.

"Why in billy heck are you kids here, anyways?" demanded Jack fiercely.

"We . . . we just came out . . . ," said Jakie miserably.

"We thought it would be all right to watch," snuffled Rose, brushing at the snow and needles that clung to her coat. Her hair was full of snow too, and her cap lay tangled in the branch that had struck her. She stopped and looked at the tree, stretched beside the cluster of stumps behind which she and Jakie had crouched.

Her stomach turned over.

"Don't faint, girlie!" she heard Army shouting at her. Her face must have been very white.

"I'm all right," she said, starting to cry. There was fear and anger and confusion mixed up inside of her and she didn't know how she felt.

For a few minutes there was a loud confusion of voices. Several other men, on their way back to the camp for dinner, stopped and lent their voices and opinions to the scene. Army, Jack, and Francis Wilson turned away to tell the story. Rose, standing still beside the stumps where she and Jakie had hidden, thought they had been forgotten and hoped they could go back home without anyone saying anything more to them. She was disappointed when Jack and Francis Wilson turned back to the children.

"Now it'll be this way, brats!" It was Jack Straws speaking. "We won't tell your pas and mas about this, but you gotta promise, and really promise, you'll never, *never* come into the pinery alone, sneakin' like that."

"Some day one o' us'll take you 'round, maybe, but ...," put in Francis Wilson.

"Oh, we promise, we promise!" they said together. "And thank you, Mr. Straws," Rose added, her eyes filling with tears again.

" 'Magine! ! Them kids was hidin' in the slashin's! Almost got kilt!" Army declaimed indignantly to the little group of watching loggers.

"Shut up, Army," said Francis Wilson. "Now, come kids, up on Sam while we go back to camp. If your innards are as hollow as mine, you kin feel the wind between your ribs!"

One by one Jakie and Rose were hoisted to the broad, bare back of the horse. Rose clutched desperately at Sam's mane, since she had never ridden without a saddle before.

On the way back to camp Rose wondered how Jakie could be so happy and joyous. The straps and fastenings of the horse's harness pinched her legs and caught her coat. Her legs ached from clinging to the huge animal and each moment she was in fear that she would fall off.

As the group moved up the broad, almost perfectly straight road toward the camp, they passed the skidway in which Rose had stood that day, weeks ago, before the cutting had started. It was almost full now of lengths of trees, their clean, pale-yellow ends looking round as plates.

The snow had covered the road, and it seemed smooth and perfect before them.

When they reached camp, Rose was lifted down from the horse, while Jakie slid down by himself and ran quickly toward the cookhouse.

"You look bad, girlie," said Jack. "Why don't you come to the cookhouse and have a cuppa tea 'fore you go home. Your ma'll see you been cryin', else."

Rose nodded and followed the group into the cookhouse. She went back to the kitchen where Nat handed her a cup of tea.

"Army told me," he whispered. "I won't tell Ma, but you gotta be good from now on." Rose nodded again, silently, and began to sip the tea. She watched the men as they ate. The tables were less than half full since only those nearest the camp came back to eat a midday meal. The others ate at their working sites, from the huge kettles that Nat had taken out late in the morning.

There was almost complete silence as the men ate, and Rose knew that no one was permitted to speak unless he wanted to ask for food to be passed. Rose thought it was just as well. She couldn't imagine wanting to eat with Army shouting in her ears, or Jack's garrulous voice going on and on with his endless stories.

The smells were wonderful, though. Steak was on the tables and huge piles of homemade bread; there were apple pies and enormous cookies laden with sugar; there were turnips and peas and fried potatoes.

When Rose had finished her tea, she stepped outdoors through the kitchen door. Nat followed her.

"Will they really keep their promise and not tell?" she asked.

Nat looked indignant. "Of course they will. See that you do, young lady. Why, do you know, you could not only have been killed, but thrashed good and hard, too!" Rose smiled and Nat glowered at her. "I mean," he went on, "they're good men and you're a lucky little girl."

"I'm *not* little," said Rose automatically. She turned to go. "I'll see you at supper time."

As she walked along the path, scuffing the new-fallen snow ahead of her, she thought about the morning and how close she and Jakie had come to real danger. She thought about how unexpected the kindness of the shanty boys had been for her, but how Nat and Jakie seemed to take it for granted. She stopped outside the door of the cabin and looked back at the cookhouse almost hidden by the fast falling snow. She remembered that she and Jakie never had reached the old camp, and she might not have reached here if. . . .

"Mother," she said, before she had closed the door, "I am going to make three pairs of mittens for some special friends of mine."

So Rose knitted mittens for Army, Jack, and Francis Wilson. They were good, thick, double-knitted grey mittens, with long wrists. At her father's suggestion, she sewed patches of deerskin in the palms. "For gripping an axe better," she told her mother. She was a fast knitter and in a week the mittens were done. "Even though your housework isn't," commented her mother sharply.

Rose knew the men had not saved her life, but she felt they had been nicer to her than she deserved, perhaps; that she had acted like a baby — in front of Jakie, too — and that they had not held it against her.

One evening, after supper, Rose stood near the bunkhouse door, waiting for her friends. When they came, wiping their mouths on their sleeves and talking loudly, she needed all her courage to beckon them to her and offer her gifts.

"Them's gorrr-geeous, Miss Rose!" exclaimed Francis Wilson, pulling his on instantly.

"Beooty-full, beooty-full," murmured Army, turning them over and gently rubbing the softness of the deerskin.

"Thanky, Miss. You're most kind," said Jack, touching his mittens to his forehead in a kind of salute.

They all thanked her over and over. She backed away from them, feeling awkward and shy. The men waved one more time and went into the close, yellow light of the bunkhouse.

The next day, as she was carrying a pail of milk from the barn to the cabin, a shanty boy approached her.

"Miss Rose," he murmured, looking around as if he were being followed, "I got only a minute, but, look, I'd be willin' to *pay* for a pair of them mittens, if you could see your way to do it for me. Name's Edward P. Jackson — they calls me Bunker. How about it, Miss?"

Rose was so surprised that she almost dropped the milk, but Bunker's huge paw shot out and saved it. She looked down and saw that the mittens he wore were the kind stocked by the van. She could see they were not as thick and roomy as the ones she had made, and Bunker's were worn and thin.

"Why . . . why, I don't know," she stammered. And she truly didn't know. The logical way out for the moment presented itself. "I'll have to ask my mother," she said with finality.

"You do that, Missy, and I hope the answer's 'yes,'" said Bunker, letting go of the pail and heading through the snow for the bunkhouse.

Rose continued toward the cabin, but met Nat, hurrying toward the cookhouse.

"What names they all have! Such queer ones! Why do they call each other things like that?" she said exuberant-

78

ly, indicating Bunker's hurrying form behind her.

"Some day I'll tell you, but not now, I'm late for work," mumbled Nat, and pushed by his sister.

"All right, all right," said Rose and skipped toward the door.

She talked long and earnestly to her mother as she swept the floor and washed the breakfast dishes. She mentioned, shyly, the money she might be able to earn. She pointed out how much more time her mother would have at this busy season, if Rose were not taking up time with schoolwork. And the big batch of yarn that was wrong for Nat's sweater anyway. She would buy it from Mrs. MacClaren, ended Rose importantly. Then she scoured the table with sand and did the same to the bottom of the black kettle that hung in the fireplace.

"Well," said Mrs. MacClaren doubtfully, "I guess it would be all right for you to start your Christmas holiday early; you may give up your studies for a few weeks, but, mind you," she said sternly, "immediately after Christmas, you will work harder than ever."

"Yes, Mama, of course, of course," said Rose.

"We must not let you go uneducated," finished her mother with a settled kind of sound to her voice.

Rose started her project that afternoon. She would make more than a pair of mittens for Bunker. She would make several pairs, maybe many, she planned enthusiastically. Maybe her father would sell them in the van! She wondered about the price, about the sizes — finally deciding simply to make them all large. The deerskin would be hard to cut, but her father had used a razor, perhaps he would let her use one, or do it for her. Or help.

She sat by the window, almost every afternoon for

almost a week, knitting by the December light, which was of a grey to match the mittens. The snow was deep this year, she had been told, and her father and Mr. Borden and all the crews were working in a kind of elation. Her mood of industry and successful activity matched theirs.

She finished Bunker's mittens on a grimly cold day. She set off at dinner time to find him, since Nat had told her he usually came into camp to eat. The wind was light but the temperature so low that it seemed to drive through her coat and sweater and dress as if she had nothing on at all. She ran across the clearing toward the kitchen house, her head down, and burying her chin, mouth, and nose in the top of her scarf. At the steps, she headed straight into Jakie.

"Ow, watch where you're going!"

"I'm sorry," chattered Rose.

"C'mon, wantcha to see somethin'."

"But I'm. . . ."

"Won't take long. C'mon." Jakie grabbed her sleeve and pulled her along. Rose sighed. How she was pushed and pulled hither and thither by Jakie.

Across the clearing, Jakie found a stump beside the road. He cleared it off with his hands, now in tattered leather mittens, and offered Rose a hand up. She clambered to the top and Jakie joined her.

They stood in silence a few minutes and then they could hear, from the woods along the road, a deep occasional shouting and a great deal of mechanical noise.

"They're coming," said Jakie.

In a few minutes Rose could see the horses, Angel and Sam, their heads bent and bobbing low, as they pulled something slowly through the woods. At first Rose could not make out what they were pulling. Then she saw a logger sitting on the front of the sleigh. Behind him was a background of huge yellow circles that rose into the air many times his height. Rose was still frowning, trying to put the picture together in her mind, when Jakie exclaimed, "Wow! That must be about the winner! Lookit that!"

And then, suddenly, Rose realized what she was seeing. The sleigh Angel and Sam were pulling along the smooth, ice-covered road was piled lengthwise with enormous logs. The pile towered above the road to a dizzy height and was wrapped around its middle with a huge chain. The shanty boy who drove the sleigh sat on a very small seat at the front and now and then he called cheerfully to the team.

"Hey-ey-ey, *up!*" he called, without impatience in his voice.

The massive load moved so smoothly in front of the watching pair that it seemed to Rose it must not be touching the ground.

"Icing makes it kind of float like that, doesn't it?" Rose was pleased to state a piece of information before Jakie did.

"Yeah," he agreed laconically.

Mr. Corot, the blacksmith, and Rose's father had joined the children at the stump.

"Think it's a record, Blackie?" asked Mr. MacClaren.

"May be, per'aps it is," answered Mr. Corot. "For a two-horse team, that is."

The group continued to watch in silence. In a few minutes the load had almost passed the camp.

"Who is driving the sleigh, Jakie?" asked Rose.

"That's Bunker Jackson, 'course."

"What!?" Rose looked in surprise at the cheerful, upright man, his face full of confidence, who drove the team with vigor and good spirits. How different from the man who had approached her so furtively and awkwardly to buy a pair of mittens only a week ago!

"That's a hard job, Rose," said her father, "he's got to know every inch of the road and every pound of his load, otherwise, well, over she goes."

"And I've seen it happen," added Blackie.

"Wow!" breathed Jakie softly.

In a few minutes, the loaded sleigh had disappeared among the trees and Rose and Jakie walked back to the cookhouse. Rose asked thoughtfully, "Does Bunker put all those logs on there himself?" Nothing would have surprised her about the man now.

" 'Course not, silly!" said Jakie. "There's a crew of loaders, peavy men, and they use a kind of hoist to get them up there. And that *is* dangerous to watch, believe me."

Rose followed Jakie into the cookhouse. She was thinking that everything around the camp seemed to be dangerous; all of the men who worked here, daring and courageous. She shook her head. It wasn't possible, they didn't look, or act, heroic most of the time. Most of them seemed poor; their clothes were shabby, their faces dirty, they scratched a lot and their language was terrible! But, Rose reflected, kicking a doormat back into place, they had always been polite and kind to her. She shook her head and closed the cookhouse door.

Rose waited in the cookhouse, helping Nat, until the men came for dinner. Before Bunker could take his place at the table, Rose ran to him and held out the mittens she had finished. She looked at him without a word. Again he was the Bunker she knew, slouched, dirty, shy.

"Thanky, Miss. Here," he added, and fumbled in his worn mackinaw, "here's the money fer 'em." He handed her a fistful of coins. She hesitated, about to refuse, about to give him the mittens in honor of his bravery, his magnificence as he drove the sleigh full of logs. But she quickly decided that to recognize him as his own man, someone who could pay his obligations, was more important.

"Thank you, Mr. Jackson," she said and took the money.

During the afternoon the wind picked up and howled in gusts around the corners. The clouds disappeared and the sun shone brightly. The trees and stumps and buildings cast lavender shadows on the snow. It was hard to go back to grey mittens. Rose thought she would take the afternoon off. She and Jakie made a slide near the cookhouse, and back and forth, almost the whole afternoon, they slid, laughing and falling from time to time. Behind the cookhouse they were protected from the wind, and until the sun dipped below the treetops, they were almost warm.

After supper that evening, her mother asked her about her project. Rose was sitting at the table with a slate and slate pencil.

"Well, Mama, I'm figuring out how to tell one pair from another. I'm working it into the pattern."

The evening wore on. Rose was drawing horses now on her slate, and looking dreamily into the fire.

"Mama," she said at last, "it's almost Christmas. I think I'd rather make Christmas presents."

Her mother nodded silently.

"Mama, is there a store someplace? I mean, not the van, but someplace I can buy Christmas gifts, for Papa and Nat?" she asked idly. "Now that I have money," she finished smugly.

"In Bay City, of course."

"But, well, how do I get there?"

"You could come with me! ?"

"With you? Are you going there?" and with increasing excitement she went on, "When, Mama? When are we going?"

"We?"

"I may, mayn't I? You said. . . ."

"I'm teasing, Rose, of course. Yes, you and I are going into town for a few days. While Mrs. Peterson has her baby. I can help with the others and she was very good to me when we first came out here and the farm was such a disappointment to your father. Yes, you may come."

"Hooray!"

"Quietly, Rose."

"I'm sorry, Mama. When will we go?"

"Not for several days. There's a good deal to do to get ready."

So, enthusiastically, Rose and her mother set about preparing to leave. Rose darned Nat's socks. Mrs. Mac-Claren baked extra bread. "Although," she said, "they'll probably eat up at the cookhouse with the shanty boys. All that heavy food. Tsk, tsk." They both swept and scrubbed and by Saturday night their bags were packed and ready. In Rose's carpetbag was the single pair of mittens she had started.

The next morning they set off early. Mr. MacClaren picked up the bags as he followed Mrs. MacClaren and Rose out of the cabin.

"Nat's gone ahead. The sleigh's at the river. He'll drive you into town and bring the sleigh back."

They walked through the almost silent camp. Down by the cookhouse, three blue jays were fighting with the pigs for the scraps that had been poured into the trough

there. Horses stamped and snorted in the stable. The
air was cold and very still.

They walked the distance to the river along the tote
road. It had not been iced since Wednesday night and
so the somewhat scarred surface was easier to walk on.

Rose had not been along this road since she and her
mother had returned triumphantly with Nat saved from
the man-catchers. Before they reached the river, they
passed the last of the trees. Rose stopped with a gasp.
The forest was gone, it seemed to her. Rolling hills of
stumps stretched almost as far as she could see. Most
places were covered with snow, but long, brown skid
trails led back through the stumps in many places. There
were many piles, large and small, of limbs, saplings,
stumps and brush, scattered over the barren land, black
against the snow.

"Did . . . did the men from Duck Tree Camp do all
of this?"

"Well, about over to, let's see, where that birch is still
standing 'way over there, and down to that stream on
this side of the road," said her father, pointing into the
distance on either side of the road. "Dunlap Camp 7 and
Obelt Camp did the rest." He continued up the road.

As the road approached the river it split into three.
One curve of the tote road went along the high banks
to the left, the other went to the right, sloping very
gently down to the lower banks. In between, the road
became only a trampled path, thick with frozen mud and
snow and rough with ice. Mr. MacClaren led them down
this path to the river.

How silent the river was, its roaring voice stilled with
ice.

"Ice is plenty firm," said Mr. MacClaren, leading

86

them out onto the ice, across the river to where Nat stood, gentling Snowball. He stepped toward them when he saw them coming.

"Up you go, Rosie," he said, helping her into the back and tucking a blanket around her knees. His mother sat beside him in the front, also bundled in blankets.

The morning sparkled in the sunlight, the river stretching white and still before them. At least, at first Rose thought it was still. Shortly she began to hear its winter voice. Sharp snaps, a groan, a creak, as if a giant lay wakefully beneath the blanket of ice and snow. She shivered and hoped the trip would be a short one.

This winter highway was a shorter route and Snowball, in her cleated shoes, seemed to trot more swiftly, drawing the hissing sleigh after her.

"What are those walls along the river bank?" asked Rose at one point.

"Walls?" asked Nat over his shoulder, and then looked at where Rose was pointing.

Across the river, right at the edge of the banks, stood high piles that looked like walls. Nat laughed.

"Those are the rollways. That's where they're taking the logs when they drive them on the sleighs down the tote road. See? They're piled against them posts in the ground."

"*Those* posts . . . ," said Mrs. MacClaren quietly.

"All right, *those* posts, then."

In some places the rollways were lower and seemed hardly like a wall at all. Mile after mile along the river, and up the banks of smaller streams that fed the river, stretched the rollways.

Sometimes the river wound through low fields and

Rose could see the very slightest mist covering the black-dotted, snow-covered lands. The horizon still gave glimpses of uncut green pines. Her heart lifted and she breathed deeply. She had grown used to the smell of freshly cut pine so gradually that most days she did not notice it at all, but this morning the fog in the air held the fresh, sharp odor and Rose felt that the air had washed her lungs.

But it was cold, and by the time they reached Bay City, Rose's fingers and feet were very cold. They left the river and took to the rutted, ice-covered road. The sleigh passed a short row of large houses, most of them set quite close to the road, with fields, and sometimes barns, stretching out behind them.

Soon they were in the center of town. The shops that lined the street were closed and shuttered. Rose thought the streets looked dirty and untidy. The snow was gone from much of the hard, rutted gravel road, and where it stayed it was covered with thick black soot. Papers and bottles lay, covered with frost, frozen hard to the snow and the street. A church bell rang crisply in the icy air and in the distance Rose could make out the jingle of sleigh bells.

Nat drove the sleigh carefully around the patches of bare road until they reached a side street, into which he guided Snowball. The street ran up a gradual hill, lined on either side with plain, grey-painted two-story houses, all set close to the street, only narrow side yards separating them. Rose was relieved. She had been afraid that they were headed for one of the shacks she and her mother had passed on her very first day in Bay City.

The Petersons lived in one of the tall, narrow houses. The porch was high and awkward looking, but to Rose, after months among the raw, crude buildings of Duck Tree Camp, it seemed like civilization again.

The Petersons — five of them were at home — met Rose and her mother and helped Nat carry their two bags into the house. Then Nat said good-bye to his mother and sister and set off in the sleigh for home.

"I hope nothing happens to him, Mama," whispered Rose, as her brother clucked to Snowball and the horse jingled back down the street. She was thinking of man-catchers and her mother seemed to understand.

"Nothing will, Rose, I'm certain," answered Mrs. MacClaren and squeezed her daughter's hand.

Emma, the Petersons' daughter, was eleven, lively and energetic. Almost like Jakie, Rose often thought. Her father and mother let her take a few days out of school to be company for Rose.

They became fast friends and Rose didn't like to think about the time when she and Emma would be separated. Rose told Emma about the man-catchers and of her determination to catch them herself and bring them to justice.

"We'll come out for the start of the drive, we always do, and. . . ."

"You mean when they send the logs down the river?" interrupted Rose.

"Yep. It's kinda like a picnic. Leastways, Pa and Jimmy and I'll come. Ma'll most likely have to stay home with the baby. Anyway, then maybe you and me can catch those kidnappers."

"Yes? Oh, yes! I'm so glad you want to help, Emma. That ol' Jakie won't do anything." And then Rose told Emma about their adventure in the woods and all the other things that had happened to her at Duck Tree Camp.

And Emma showed Rose around town. Soon Rose knew it almost as well as Emma did.

After the pretty shops and tearooms she had known at her grandmother's, the dry-goods stores and general stores of the lumbering town seemed barren and crude,

but Rose found herself interested and excited after the long months at Duck Tree Camp. She bought a pipe for her father and earmuffs for Nat. For her mother she chose a china vase, shaped like a lady's slipper.

Finally, one morning at breakfast, Mr. Peterson said that Emma had to return to school.

"You'll find things to do, Rose," he said kindly.

"You'll have to amuse yourself, Rose. I must stay here. Meg may have her baby any minute," Mrs. MacClaren added.

"Go down to the piers and look at the ships tied up there for the winter. The last one came up the river a week ago," suggested Emma.

In answer to Mrs. MacClaren's worried look, Mr. Peterson said, "There's not much of anybody there to bother her, ma'm. Just old Higgy, and he won't bother her." He put down the spoon with which he had been eating his oatmeal. "I think it's real interesting to see the river all froze and piled with ice," he said sheepishly.

"Well, I guess it would be all right," said Mrs. Mac-Claren.

Rose gave an excited bounce.

Later that morning, she left the lonesome house and started up the street.

"I'll be back for dinner right at noon, Mama!" she called to her mother, who stood on the little porch waving to her.

10 Ghosts

Rose set off down the main street. She walked for several blocks, going slowly and looking in the store windows and up the side streets. She walked softly, too. The town was very quiet and frozen, locked in the winter as was the river over which she had come to the city. How different from a farming town, where the winter stilled the countryside and the town would be full of socials and prayer meetings and school recitations. The shanty boys weren't allowed to come into town much at all, she knew. Their bosses were afraid of whiskey and other things. Rose shivered deliciously and skipped softly on her way.

She stopped at the edge of the lumber-mill yard and watched and listened for a long time. The smell of pine was even stronger here than in the woods. There were careless piles of uncut logs lying at one end of the building; at the other, on the pier, were a few piles of cut lumber. By standing on tiptoe and looking through a gap in the collection of gray buildings, Rose could see the river beyond. Here and there in the ice she could make out the darkness of a log or two, frozen tight, caught in the boom now till spring, or a thaw.

She walked on, passing more docks that jutted into the tumbled ice of the river. She finally reached a place where the pier seemed to end. The banks of the river curved widely beyond and far away in the frozen landscape and finally became the shores of Saginaw Bay. Here and there along the shore she could make out small boats drawn onto land for the winter. But most of the world seemed covered with ice, from here. The river was still open a little here, so near the bay, but she had to stand on a piling and peer over moving mounds of ice to see the stream.

"If you look real hard — on a clear day. . . ." Rose jumped and whirled around as a voice spoke behind her. It was an old man, tall, with broad shoulders and a bright red cap on his head.

"As I was sayin', if you look real hard — on a clear day — you kin still see some lake water, too." The man paused to light a pipe and then went on, "Won't be for long, though. Few more days of hard winter like this, and the bay'll be solid ice too, 'most a month early this year." He stopped again, and Rose looked back at him. He was squinting at the horizon, although the Bay was too far away to see. Rose felt as if she had been tied to the spot, that she must not make a sound until the old man had finished what he had to say. Finally, he spoke again. "Then, then, it's toss ice blocks up on the shore, big as houses, some of 'em." This was said with such grim force that Rose could not help gasping.

The man looked at her and smiled slightly.

"Where ya' from, little girl?" he asked in a very ordinary tone of voice.

94

"Well, I, uh, my papa," began Rose confusedly, "he's up at Duck Tree Camp. We're — Mama and me — we're just visiting."

"Hmm. You must be the Eastern girl then."

"Yes! But how did you know?" asked Rose.

"Oh, we hear things, us here at the docks." He puffed some more on his pipe and then took it out of his mouth. Again, Rose felt that somehow, without words, she had been commanded to be silent. She turned again toward the mouth of the river. Near the horizon the clear blue of the sky was darker, mistier, and it was hard to tell where the ice began. The sun, high in the sky, looked very cold to Rose and a small gust of wind from off the lake made her shiver.

"Yup, we hear lots of things," said the old man. Don't suppose you've seen anyone walkin' around on the ice today."

"Why, no," said Rose. "But I just got here."

Rose didn't think he heard her, but she waited for what he would say next. Far off she could hear the high screech of a saw at the mill. Blocks of ice crunched and banged under the end of the pier.

"Well, it don't matter. I've seen 'em walking, I have." His voice was deep and slow now.

Rose asked, "Who? Who did you see?"

Very slowly, the old man turned and looked down at Rose. "The dead. They as is gone beyond." Rose gulped.

Then, with another change in his tone, the tension relaxed and the man motioned to a row of low kegs that were lined up behind them. "Sit down, girl — what's your name? — and I'll tell you all about it."

"I'm Rose MacClaren."

"Glad to meet ya'. I'm Higgins, they call me Old Higgy," he said and chuckled. "Sit down, sit down!"

95

Rose couldn't help smiling back at Old Higgy and, without even looking at its top, sat down on the keg.

Old Higgy took another match from his trousers pocket and again set out to light his pipe. It took him a few minutes and Rose saw his eyes stray continuously toward the horizon as he puffed. Finally, he seemed satisfied with the fire.

"Well, it was this way. Musta been, oh, ten, twelve years ago, the *Minnie J. Ellsworth* — she was a schooner, outta Detroit — was on her way to Chicago, only it was late in the season, real late, almost the middle of December. Her captain had almost decided not to go, but there was a load of immigrants and they was real anxious to get to Chicago for Christmas, so they could have the winter to get their gear together, so come spring, they could push on to Montana. Anyway, they was willing to pay extra and the captain had a pretty little wife that needed new dresses and such, so he went ahead and sailed anyhow. One thing after another happened, though. His cook was killed in a brawl before they got halfway up the St. Clair, and they had to put in at Marine City and was there three or four days before they got another. Coming out of the river is bad in any weather, and it was foggy and black as pitch when they hit the lake. Before they'd gone more'n a mile or two, the first accident happened. They came around another schooner, loaded with lumber, only what they couldn't see, and didn't know, was that she was pulling four rafts behind her. The *Minnie J. Ellsworth* cut the rope between the schooner and the first barge — cut it, fortunately for her. The schooner was pulled 'round some, but nothing much happened to her, but the waves was running high and it was pitch dark, like I said. The other captain didn't have a chance to get his rafts back.

96

Only trouble was, they was three or four men on each raft and it looked to the captain of the lumber ship as if the first barge had gone over. As it turned out — though nobody knew this for some time to come — the captain of the *Minnie J.* had picked up most of the crew from the overturned raft."

He stopped and puffed on his pipe, applying another match finally. Rose made little prodding, questioning noises to get him going again.

"As for the other rafts, they washed up in different places, some on the Canadian side. The crews aboard them — there were three rafts still floating — were cold and hungry, I guess, but all right otherwise." He stopped again and sat gazing at the horizon.

"But what about the *Minnie J?* Don't stop now," said Rose.

"Oh, the *Minnie J.* Well, she went on, up the coast, 'round the thumb and headed into the bay here. Soon as she passed Fish Point, dropped her anchor and lowered her sails. The wind was fierce and the ice had already started to pile up along the shore and she wasn't sure she could make it into the river mouth. We know all this, 'cause she put out a boat and it took 'most all day, but the boat reached Bay City around nightfall — they walked across the ice the last mile or so — and the boatmen told us. Well, a bunch of men from the town set out to get to the *Minnie J.;* they all just thought they'd bring back the survivors from the raft. But we wasn't. . . ."

"You were with them?" breathed Rose.

"Oh, yes. We wasn't more'n a quarter of the way there when the storm began. Mostly it was wind, the coldest wind I've ever felt, but there was ice and snow in 'er, too. Well, we had to wait out the storm. Three days she blew, the temperature goin' lower every minute. By the time she blew out, the bay was froze as far out as we could see. We thought maybe the *Minnie J.* could ride out the storm, and if she could, she'd be frozen in. We went to the place where she shoulda been, but not a sight of her. Gone, she was, hull, masts, and sails. There wasn't anything to do but go home, which we did." He stopped abruptly this time and knocked his pipe against the keg next to him, the black lumps of tobacco falling to the pier. Rose was certain this was not the end of the story, but somehow she knew he didn't want to be urged on this time. She sat quietly while he pulled on a pair of tattered mittens.

"So. A month went by, maybe a month and a half.

The bay was frozen solid. Ice fishermen said thickest they'd seen in years. One evening Miz Olson, who lives up near the mouth of the river, only a few hundred feet from the beach — lonely sorta spot in the winter, I tell you — she looks out her door and with the sun, almost down behind the hills, at her back, she saw people walking across the ice! Clear as you and me, she said they was. A man, tall and young, helping a young woman, bundled up in shawls and a bonnet, was coming with two other men, one short and the other medium, behind him. Well, Miz Olson thought right off they was survivors from the *Minnie J.* She said later no other thought even crossed her mind, though goodness knows nobody really thought the ship had gone down, only that the

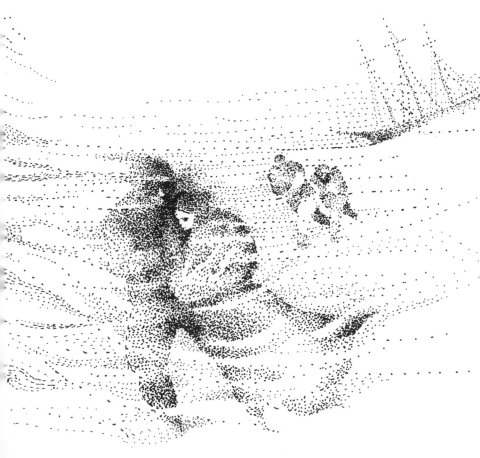

captain had decided to go on. And they was enough
other reasons why such a group could be comin' over the
ice. But, no, says Miz Olson, she knew right off they was
from the *Minnie J.* So, she put on the coffeepot and
threw another two logs on the fire — she knew what
they'd want — and then set to the barn for Olson himself and told him to go meet them. The sun had gone
clear down by that time, and when he walked out from
the beach — climbing fierce piles of ice, let me tell you
— there wasn't no sign of them. Well, that wasn't so
queer, could of been they'd cut over the other way and
headed up the river. Miz Olson said it seemed odd, but
she thought no more about it.

"Next evening, Miz Olson looks out her door again,
and . . . what do you suppose she saw?" He stopped and,
turning his head slowly, looked at Rose with a piercing
gaze. Mutely, Rose shook her head and shivered. Old
Higgy turned his head again toward the distant bay and
continued. "Well, she saw the same group of people —
the man, holding the woman, the others behind. Olson
was right there in the kitchen with her and he quick
put on his mackinaw and mittens and set off to the
beach. Again, before he could climb the ice piles on the
shore, they was gone. Miz Olson, who didn't leave the
door the whole time, said a kind of gust of fog and snow
came up and when it had settled down, there wasn't no
group there. To make a long story short, the same group
appeared three more nights running and then, well, they
just stopped coming. For that year. Next year, same time
of February, same time of the day, Miz Olson seen 'em
again and this time Miz Rafferty and old lady Gotwash
was with her, so — aside from old lady Gotwash, who'd
swear to anything for a cut of tobacco — everybody knew
then that the Olsons hadn't been makin' it up."

100

"Do they still come?" asked Rose.

"Oh, sure," said Old Higgy nonchalantly. "Every few years some farm boy, or Indian, or ice fisherman catches sight of them. Always the same group."

"Who are they, do you think?" asked Rose.

"Well, we can't know for sure, since they don't talk much." Here he stopped and roared with laughter, and then went on. "But we did find out what happened to the *Minnie J*. She was washed up, intact, near Thunder Bay, north of here. There wasn't nobody on board her and not one of the crew or passengers ever showed up — 'ceptin', of course, the three or four that came in for help at the first." He stopped, put the pipe in his pocket and slapped his knees as if he intended leaving.

Rose wanted to hear more about the *Minnie J*. She could see herself now telling Jakie and Nat. She put a hand on Higgy's arm. "So those people they saw were ghosts?"

"Think what you like," said Higgy. Rose could see that he wanted to go on. She shook his arm very slightly and he continued. "They think most likely the ship froze up tight during that storm, so the passengers and crew set out to walk to land. But it's a long way, with women and children and no proper sleds, I 'spect. In a day or so ther'd have been some open water again, most likely. Then, if there was fog, they coulda lost their direction. A peddler from Detroit was through the spring after Miz Olson, Miz Rafferty and old lady Got-wash seen 'em and he said the young woman sounded a lot like the captain's new bride — he'd read about the *Minnie J*. in the Detroit newspaper."

"And they never found anybody?" persisted Rose.

"Nope." Now she could tell he was through. He

slapped his knees again and rose from the keg. "Gettin'
on fer dinner time, Miss. You better think about goin'
home."

"Yes, yes," said Rose absently. She looked up at him.
"Thank you for the story. I enjoyed it very much." She
extended her hand and, surprised, Old Higgy took the
mittened fingers gingerly and shook them once.

"You're more'n welcome. Come again." He touched
his cap.

"Good-bye," said Rose and walked quickly back up
the pier, not looking back, thinking hard about what
she had heard. She was sure her mother would consider
it a "bad influence," so she decided right then never to
tell it in her mother's presence. She did decide, smugly,
to thrill Emma with the tale.

She turned into the Peterson gate just as the noon
whistle at the lumber mill blew.

Her mother came to the door and called out just as
Rose started up the steps.

"Come in, come! The Petersons have a new baby boy!
And they're going to name it after your father!"

Rose clapped her hands. She could see how pleased
her mother was and she knew her father would be, too.
This meant they'd be starting back to Duck Tree Camp
in a few days. She wouldn't be able to share a real bed
and mattress with Emma any more; or sit in a real par-
lor; or walk down real streets and see stores, actual stores!
But life seemed slower here, dead and suspended compared to the strong flow of excitement in the lumber camp.
The weather was dull and cold there, the cabin cramped
and dingy, but in spite of it all, Rose felt almost as if it
would be like waking from a ghostly sleep to comfortable,
bustling familiarity to return to Duck Tree Camp.

102

11 Christmas

And now it was almost Christmas, the time of year Rose loved best. In the cabin, her mother was making puddings and pies; there was something in her mother's knitting bag she knew she shouldn't see; and carefully hidden in her end of the attic were the presents she had spent all her money for in Bay City. The cabin seemed cozy and shining, more and more as if she had spent all her life there.

On Christmas Eve day, Rose looked out of the window across the drifted, blown snow and saw the loggers returning from the woods for dinner, their mackinaws crusted with snow and their beards laced with white.

"You should get some fresh air and exercise, Rose," said her mother from just behind her.

"But I like it in here. . . ."

"Rose, you're looking pale," said Mrs. MacClaren energetically. "You need the air." She reached over and took Rose's jacket and scarf from their hook beside the door.

"Well, all right," said Rose tiredly. "I can go over and see Jakie."

"That's a fine idea." Something in her mother's voice made Rose pause slightly and then brighten, but she said nothing more than, "Well, I'll be home after a while."

Snow filled the air and Rose fought her way against the wind to the cookhouse. Nat was there, perhaps he'd let her in for a while, and maybe Jakie would be there and they could find something to do.

A cloud of steam and lovely odors surrounded her in the doorway as she entered. Nat was stirring a huge pot while Mr. O'Connor stood at the oven, the door open, ladling drippings over half a dozen gently browning geese. Loaves of bread were lined up on the table, and dozens of mince and pumpkin pies stood there too. Rose had eaten a short time before, but her mouth watered at the smells and sights.

"Rose, you'll have to leave!" shouted Nat, raising his voice above the sizzle of the geese and murmuring roar of the pot he was stirring.

"Why?" she asked.

"We're too busy to have you here. Men have their Christmas dinner tonight."

" 'Lo," said a voice at her shoulder. She turned to find Jakie behind her, motioning her to follow him out the open door.

"Heard you spent a week in town," said Jakie as they kicked a path through the snow toward the blacksmith shop. Rose could always be sure Jakie would head there. She, too, enjoyed the warmth and the glow of the fire.

104

"Let's go talk to Jimmy Palmer!" he called to Rose above the howl of the wind.

Rose said nothing, but waited until they were sheltered inside the blacksmith shop.

"Who's Jimmy Palmer?" she asked as the door closed behind them.

"That's me, Miss," said a hearty voice from near the furnace.

Rose and Jakie peered at a strangely dressed figure sitting in the gloom. He wore, as did all woodsmen, a heavy mackinaw, dingy trousers, a knitted hat, but over his mackinaw were tied red and purple and yellow scarves, with another gaily encircling the hat. Another scarf appeared to be tied around his waist, because its ends dangled richly below the bottom of his mackinaw.

"Jimmy plays the fiddle, don't you?" asked Jakie, turning from Rose to the stranger.

"That's right, songs and dances," and he smiled up at the children.

Behind them, Mr. Corot — Blackie — began banging on a horseshoe. Jimmy Palmer tapped his foot to the rhythm.

"Always music in a blacksmith's shop, young ones," he said with a laugh.

"Are you going to play here?" asked Rose.

"Not here, dummy, in the bunkhouse, tonight," said Jakie.

"That's what I meant. Here in camp," said Rose hurriedly.

"Yep. I'm gonna bring 'em a little Christmas cheer."

Mr. Corot stopped his work.

"Better git over to the cookhouse, Jimmy. They'd give you a bite to tide you over."

105

"Oh, yes," said Rose hospitably. "My brother works over there."

"Humph," said Jakie with authority, "my pa *runs* the cookhouse. Let's go."

Jimmy Palmer rose, and picked up a battered violin case and a small bundle. He followed the two children back across the howling camp. Inside the cookhouse, he talked with Mr. O'Connor for a few minutes and put his bag and violin case down while he sat at the table. Rose and Jakie sat on either side of him. There were plates of cookies and doughnuts, a basket of apples and a plate of ham — the usual food for eating between meals. "Loggers never seem to get enough to eat," Jakie was always saying. Nat brought Jimmy Palmer a cup of tea and sat down opposite.

"Where you from?" asked Nat.

"I'm from Maine, young feller. A hard country. I'm here to earn some money for my family. I ain't a fisherman, like most back home. I'm a farmer. . . ."

"So is Papa," put in Rose.

"Yes. And in the winter he's got to do something else, that right? So. I take my violin and play for little bits of money here and there. This year I played on the steamship that goes to Chicago and now I'm on my way back to Maine, playin' in camps like this." He stopped talking abruptly and helped himself to two more doughnuts and then leaned back, smiling at the children.

The three young people stared back at him in silence. Rose could think of many things to ask him, but shyness held her back. How romantic it would have seemed to her a few months ago, traveling everywhere, making beautiful music, but now, she had ridden the steamship, she had lived in the logging camp and knew the rough frontier towns. She thought Jimmy Palmer's life must be very hard.

"Nat was kidnapped," inserted Jakie. Trying to make conversation, Rose thought.

"That so? Man-catchers, eh?" His words seemed nonchalant, but Rose could sense that he was really interested.

"Yep," answered Nat, also with nonchalance.

"Hmmm. One of 'em a big, red-bearded feller?"

"Yes, that's right! Do you know them?" asked Rose excitedly.

"Well, Miss, I seen 'em, I guess." He fell silent and went on eating.

"Where, where?" urged Jakie.

"Now, hold still, youngster, let me think," said Jimmy Palmer.

He continued eating thoughtfully, while Nat, Rose, and Jakie waited without moving or breathing. After a moment he wiped his mouth on his hand and looked up.

"Reckon he's out in the pines by now, but last time I saw him was only a couple of weeks ago, downriver. He looked a mighty unpleasant customer, so I sneaked on by without sayin' 'howdy.' He was pulling some fish up from a hole in the ice, and gettin' ready to head for the tall timber, I guess."

Jakie and Rose looked at each other, excitedly.

"He's *not* gone . . . ," said Jakie.

"We could catch him," finished Rose.

"Hey, now hold on a bit there, young'uns. It's not that simple."

"No, sir, Rose," said Nat angrily, "you promised you wouldn't do anything like that."

107

Rose looked taken aback; she lowered her head and nodded, dumbly.

"Oh, we won't," said Jakie. "Leastways not 'til spring."

"Not ever," said Nat sternly, and Rose pulled on Jakie's jacket gently, shaking her head very slightly when he turned toward her.

"That's right, children," said Jimmy Palmer cheerily, "better leave well enough alone. They're tough customers, man-catchers."

Nat and the fiddler began to talk of other things. They talked of the weather, and whether the spring drive would be a good one and the temper of the shanty boys this Christmas. Then Mr. O'Connor began to rattle the pot lids.

"Well, I guess I gotta get to work," said Nat and went back to his pot, with his huge wooden spoon.

Jimmy Palmer grabbed one more doughnut and rose.

"And I'd better get to the bunkhouse and find me a corner. Gotta be ready for the celebration!" He laughed but Rose somehow thought he didn't mean it.

"I'll show you where, Jimmy," said Jakie, scrambling off the bench. Rose started after them, but stopped in the door when Jakie called to her. "You can't come! It's the bunkhouse, 'n' just for men!" She stuck out her tongue at him, but only after his back was turned again. She sniffed the browning geese once more and closed the door behind her.

* * * *

That night Rose helped Nat in the kitchen as supper was being served. Her mother didn't really approve, but Rose had concluded that Mrs. MacClaren must have wanted her out of the house for a while and she went eagerly when her brother asked.

She had never been in the cookhouse during an evening meal before. It was so much quieter than she had expected. Somehow she had not believed the silence could be so complete. Only the shuffle of feet, the rattle of tableware, and an occasional mutter of "Taters," or "Bread," were heard. Nat and Jake, as if under the same law, were silent, too, as they carried food and dishes back and forth from the kitchen. Once, as she stood slicing bread in a corner near the stove, Rose whispered to her brother, "Won't you even let them talk on Christmas Eve?"

Nat glanced at Jake, who was pushing two pies onto a farther table, and then answered in a whisper, "It's even worse then, he says. More apt to get outta hand than during regular time. . . ." He stopped as he saw Jake frown at them. "Tell you later," he muttered, then turned to a huge wooden tub and began digging from it chunks of butter and slapping them into bowls. "Butter," called one of the men and Nat hurried into the dining area with two bowls in his hands.

At last the meal was over, and Rose and Nat and Jake had finished washing the dishes, with Jakie taking the piles of warm tin plates and setting the table all over again for the morning meal.

Nat tugged on his boots, Rose pulled on her mittens, and they stepped into the cold dark.

"It's stopped snowing! And look at the stars!" said Rose, standing in the path with her head thrown back.

"Yeah," answered Nat.

"You were going to tell me why the men can't talk."

"Oh. Yeah. . . ."

"You should say 'yes,' not 'yeah,' " said Rose virtuously, "you know how Mama hates slangy words."

109

"Yes, ma'm," Nat answered with an exaggerated hiss. "Go on."

"Would you rather give me a grammar lesson?" Nat stopped to make a snowball and throw it toward a pine tree at the nearer edge of the camp.

"Tell me, Nat!"

"Well, they usually can't talk at meals in lumber camps, 'cause they fight easy and if they can't say anything it cuts down on the chance of fights."

"But on Christmas. . . ."

"What's Christmas to them," interrupted Nat, " 'ceptin' being away from their families, most of 'em, and sometimes an extra day off, so the boss kin go to church." He picked up a handful of snow and threw it at a stump.

"Why don't they go to see their families?"

"Won't let 'em," said Nat flatly.

"Why?" Rose was indignant at the plight of her friends.

" 'Cause they'll get drunk," said Nat bluntly.

"Nat! How awful!"

"It's true. That's why they can't go to town, either. Borden's pretty strict, but not any stricter than other bosses."

They walked in silence for a few minutes, going very slowly, letting the quiet dark sink into their minds, looking now and then at the sparkling sky. Nat stopped suddenly and grabbed Rose's arm. He pointed. Rose could make out among the trees just beyond the bunkhouse a dark figure, quickly disappearing into the forest. She could not tell who it was, but she could see the white circle of his face from time to time as he looked back over his shoulder.

110

"Who's that?" she asked when he had gone out of sight.

"Dunno, but I know where he's goin' and why." Nat threw a giant handful of snow into the air and it fell back on them in little lumps.

"Tell me, tell me, Nat."

"Oh, I s'pect he's going into town to get some liquor for the rest."

"Nat! Shouldn't we tell?"

"Who? Pa? You want him stumbling around in the woods on Christmas Eve? Or Borden? He's gone to church, won't be back 'til Monday. Nobody else would care." Nat spoke belligerently and Rose could see that he didn't really want anyone to go after the shanty boy.

She did not answer. They went on walking past the bunkhouse.

The door opened and someone threw a bucket of water out, to one side of the path. Rose could see into the dimly lighted room beyond. The air was cloudy with smoke and dim in the crowded space.

"Who'd be merry in a place like that!" said Nat.

"Mr. Palmer will help, won't he? Playing and all?"

"Oh, he'll help all right. They'll have a good time, but. . . ." Nat threw another snowball.

As he finished speaking, the sound of a violin floated out to them. Nat went to the small window nearest them, plowing over his boot tops through the snow. He peered in for a minute, then motioned to Rose.

"No," she whispered and stayed where she was.

In a few minutes Nat joined her. "Why didn't you look? They were just dancing. And your friend Jimmy Palmer was playing for them."

"I don't know," said Rose frowning. "It didn't seem

111

right. It's like they were animals in a cage, or something." She started walking toward home again, striding purposefully now. "Besides, they don't peek at me."

A moo sounded suddenly from behind the closed doors of the barn. A mass of snow swished down through the branches of the pine tree. Nat watched Rose a moment and then followed her again.

"Merry Christmas, children!" said their mother as the door opened. Rose and Nat stood crowded together in the doorway, looking into their cabin. Three paper roses held a green garland across the front of the fireplace and two silver candlesticks — not new — burned on the table. Mama and Papa, their faces ruddy, lighted and shadowed in the firelight, smiled a special welcome.

A dry branch blew across the door as Rose closed it behind her.

to booming grounds

BB

lumber

gap men

boomsticks

"His foot slipped and into
the water he fell."
Chapter XVII

12 Thaw

For two days it had been sleeting and raining and snowing, then freezing and thawing for an hour or two. Snow-crusted ice hung from the eaves, looking ready to fall, but now suspended in space.

"Only two weeks after Christmas and it already seems as if it had never been." Rose murmured this aloud as she sat listlessly by the kitchen window. Her mother had gone to see Mrs. O'Connor. Nat was working and even Jakie was busy today, carrying chunks of hardwood for the blacksmith's fire. Rose sighed and rubbed at the steam on the inside of the window. "How can any place be as dull as this one!" she said pettishly to herself.

Mrs. MacClaren had asked Rose to come with her. Mrs. O'Connor was sewing baby clothes — it wouldn't be long now, Rose's mother had said — but the paths were so slippery that Rose didn't feel like working up the energy to go. Now, two hours later, she wished she had. She had written a letter to her grandmother; she had mended her stockings; she'd set the bread for its second rising; and she'd finished — for the third time — the book she had been given for Christmas.

Suddenly she stood up. "I'll go find Jakie. I can even watch him work. That's better than staying here." With energy she put on her wraps and in a few minutes was sliding over the ground toward the blacksmith's, its fevered heart shining through the gray day.

"Mizzuble day!" said Blackie, greeting her. "They's more shanty boys fallin' and rollin' around in the timber than they is logs, today." Rose looked timidly around. She and Blackie were alone in the shop. His remark gave her courage to ask a question that had been in her mind for a whole day, ever since the ice storm began the day before.

"I thought you'd all like the ice storm. Don't they ice the roads to haul the logs?"

"Yep. But the ice don't belong on the trees and the stumps and around where a body's tryin' to swing an axe and can't hardly stand up. Why, some of the boys put on their caulked boots for the day!"

"Caulked?" murmured Rose questioningly. The blacksmith loved to talk and Rose knew he'd tell her what the word meant.

"Yep. Boots with spikes on 'em. Both the horses and the men wear 'em. Nasty devils," he interrupted himself and, suddenly wiping the back of it on his shirt, he thrust his left hand out at Rose. It was covered with black spots. "Logger's smallpox. Reached too fast fer another feller's peavy." With an air of satisfaction he pushed some snuff up his nose.

114

"What . . . what do you mean?" asked Rose apprehensively.

"Stepped on it with his caulked boots, hard as he could."

"Goodness!"

Blackie cackled and sneezed and then turned back to the forge.

"Makin' . . . another . . . branding . . . hammer . . . fer . . . yore . . . paw," he said, between strokes of his hammer.

"Oh," Rose looked closely, but she couldn't make out what it was going to be. "What does he do with it?"

"He'll be markin' the ends of the logs, as he counts 'em, so's we can tell our own when the drive starts."

Rose decided this was too much information to gather all at once and so she changed the subject. "Where's Jakie?"

"Sent him down to the river, to yore paw to find out how long a handle I should put on this critter."

"I think I'll go find him," said Rose, and edged out of the smithy.

"So long, girlie!" called Blackie, "take it easy and don't slide into the river!" He roared with laughter as Rose walked timidly across the camp, skittering now and then on a badly iced patch of snowy ground. She walked out the end of the camp nearest the river and started up the wide, straight road in search of Jakie. A few steps told her the road was impossibly slippery. "I need caulked boots," she muttered to herself. "No wonder Sam wears them. How awful! He can't take his shoes off at night," and Rose giggled at the idea.

All around her the iced trees rattled and swished gently. Now and then, with a great rattle and swoosh,

115

pieces of ice showered from a branch shaking itself free. Once, a crack, like a shot, rang through the woods and Rose saw a limb suddenly hanging loose and free, broken by the weight of the ice.

In a few minutes Rose emerged on the road at the river bank. Loud voices attracted her attention a few hundred feet to the left. A loaded sleigh stood there. The enormously towering load of logs appeared even higher and more precarious here in the open. The driver was sitting proudly on his perch, but Rose could see her father and three other men arguing violently near a low pile of logs stacked against poles at the very edge of the river bank. She walked slowly and as unobtrusively as possible toward them. The path here was icy, too, but broken by ruts so that the walking was easier. The path to her father was gradually uphill, and when she thought of slipping and falling into the ice-covered stream below, Rose was glad to see the piles of logs that lined the river bank.

None of the four men standing paid any attention to Rose, but the driver touched his forehead and smiled at her.

"Hello, Mr. Jackson," she said politely. Then she turned her attention to the quarreling men.

"What are they arguing about?" she asked Bunker in a loud whisper.

"Heh, heh! Ol' Borden wants 'em to unload these here logs but yore paw and Francis Wilson says if'n they do today, with the rollways covered with ice, somebody'll get kilt."

"Borden, you can't ask them to take that chance!" shouted Mr. MacClaren.

"MacClaren, you're the scaler here and if you wanna

116

stay one, you mind yore brandin' hammer. Look here, Francis Wilson," he went on, turning to the huge blond man, "you and Jack's the best peavy men I got. You kin handle 'er." Rose thought it sounded as if he were pleading with Francis Wilson.

"Maybe, Mr. Borden. Maybe. Probably could in fact, but it's too chancy. What's the hurry?"

"Yeah, Borden, wait a coupla hours," said Rose's father.

"We ain't got a coupla hours!" he shouted. "I got bosses, too, ya know!"

"Nope, we won't do it, Mr. Borden, sir." Francis Wilson stuck his peavy decidedly under his arm. "I might not git hurt, 'cause I work the up end of the log, but Jack here, workin' the down end, could knock him like a billiard ball into the river." Jack looked at Francis Wilson with relief and gratitude on his face.

Mr. Borden stamped right up to Francis Wilson, the top of his head level with the logger's chin. With apoplectic rage he said, "You ornery, no-good shanty boy, take that peavy and git to work!"

"Talk to him, Mr. MacClaren," appealed Francis Wilson.

Rose's father had stepped over to the rollway pile in question.

"Look, here, Borden!" he said exultantly. "Temperature's gone up. Look at that!" He pointed to the logs in the rollways. Rose was puzzled as Mr. Borden ran his bare hand over the nearest log.

"Hmmm. Wet," he said. "Well, you're lucky, Francis Wilson, that I didn't take it outta your pay. The ice'll be gone in a coupla hours."

Borden stamped away without another word. It left

Rose wondering what they would do, but the men seemed to understand. Bunker slid down and draped the reins loosely around a post sticking up from the end of his wagon. Aside to Rose he rasped, "If he'd taken anything outta Francis Wilson's pay, Francis Wilson'd take it outta his hide." He snickered.

Rose smiled and then said, "Where's Jakie? Blackie said he was here."

"Oh, I seen him on his way back to camp as I passed with this here load." Bunker spit across the road.

"Rose!" She turned quickly at the sound of her father's voice. "What are you doing here?" He looked fiercely angry.

"I . . . I just came to find Jakie, Papa."

"He's been gone from here for ten minutes. Now, listen to me, daughter. You're not to come down here. Not during the winter, anyway. You can come to the spring breakaway with everyone else, but not now. It's just lucky today they can't unload for a bit or you might have been hurt, bad." He seemed very angry and Rose was abashed and a little angry herself. She didn't like to be scolded so completely in front of the three shanty boys.

But she knew what she was supposed to say, so she hung her head and said, softly, "I'm sorry, Papa. I didn't know." It worked as she knew it would.

"Well, see that you don't again," said Mr. MacClaren in a softer, forgiving tone.

"What's that, Papa?" said Rose. She pointed to a shining instrument standing against the end of the rollway.

"That's a branding hammer."

"What do you do with it?"

"Rose, you're wasting time. I want you to go home,

118

you know that. Now, I'll walk back a little with you. Come on." He started up the river bank toward the point at which the tote road entered the forest. Suddenly, as they passed a half-full rollway, he stopped.

"Here. See, Rose? This is what I do with the branding hammer, I make these marks on the ends of the logs." He pointed to the pale yellow of a cut log end. "I just hammer it in, on both ends. . . ."

"But why?" Rose interrupted.

"Let me tell you. Because in the spring we send all the logs down the river to the town and all the other companies do the same and they're all in there together, so when they get to the end of the river, they're separated again, and if there's no mark on a log, why, they don't know who it belongs to. Each company has its own mark, different but something like this."

Rose nodded and followed her father to the edge of the woods.

"Yep, it's melting fast," said her father. Rose could see small puddles forming on the surface of the road, and in the woods the trees were dripping now, instead of rattling. "Well, I hope it knows when to stop. We don't need a thaw!" He said this last most emphatically

and, strangely, it made Rose shiver.

By the time she reached camp and met Jakie coming across the clearing, her boots were splashing noticeably on the ice-covered road and the trees were black again, their jewelry of glittering ice gone.

"It's gonna thaw, you wait and see!" shouted Jakie.

"That's bad, isn't it?" said Rose.

"You bet!"

"Tsk. Such language. Why is it bad?" she asked.

" 'Cause they can't move any logs, 'course. Could use Big Wheels, but we ain't got none here."

Rose looked speculatively at Jakie. "Jakie, you sort of enjoy troubles, don't you?"

"Well, why not? Otherwise, it's dull here. Ma's sick all the time, waitin' for the baby. . . ."

"Jakie! Nice people don't talk about such things!"

"Then I guess I ain't nice people!" said Jakie defiantly. He was pouting and looking unhappy. Rose felt sorry for him, and the rest of the afternoon she made a special effort to try and help him feel better. She remembered the Petersons' baby and hoped for Jakie's sake that Mrs. O'Connor's baby would be happier.

Jakie's unspoken wish did come true. It did thaw. For a whole day and night the temperature climbed. When Rose stepped out to feed the chickens the next morning, she could almost smell spring in the air. "It's a long way off! I hope," said her father. But still, the smell was there, and the wet lively breeze felt like April, not January. The first day, only a few of the men stayed in camp, but by the third day of the thaw only the fallers were working. Rose could hear bickering on the steps of the bunkhouse. She wondered why they didn't go into town.

120

"Borden won't let 'em," answered Jakie, as they sat on the kitchen stoop watching Junction and Francis Wilson start to build a huge fire in front of the bunkhouse.

"Why are they doing that?" Rose finally asked.

"They're gonna wash their socks, I reckon."

Just then Mr. O'Connor put his head out the door and said in a strange voice, "Go get your mother, Rose. Quick!" Rose looked at him for a second with wide eyes and then sprang to her feet.

"Mama, Mama!" she called when she was still several yards from the cabin. "Mama!" and as she burst into the room, "It's Mrs. O'Connor! Come quick!" Without a word Mrs. MacClaren threw a shawl over her shoulders and picked up a small satchel.

Rose followed, trotting, as they went back to the cookhouse.

The next few minutes were confused and chaotic, as Rose stood in the kitchen watching her mother and Mr. O'Connor give each other terse commands. Finally, she was alone in the kitchen. Nat was chopping firewood for the kitchen range, a job that never seemed to end, and Jakie had disappeared. Rose suspected he might be in the woods, crying perhaps. She decided not to look for him. Instead, she glanced around the kitchen, thinking how close it was to dinner time and perhaps there was something she could do to help. A huge, steaming pot muttered very softly on the rear of one of the stoves. Tentatively she picked up a wooden spoon lying nearby, but then put it down again without lifting the lid of the pot.

Crash! Nat came into the kitchen, his arms full of wood.

"Shhh!" said Rose crossly.

121

"What's the matter with you?" said Nat loudly and belligerently. He dumped his armload in the woodbox.

"Mrs. O'Connor's having her baby," said Rose in a self-important way.

"Oh," said Nat, still angrily, but Rose could see that he now felt he had done something wrong and felt guilty about it. Tolerantly, she thought she should make him feel better.

"Can't I help get dinner for the men?" she asked, but Nat said nothing. "Mr. O'Connor probably won't be able to help today."

"Well . . . all right. Slice bread, will you?"

Rose looked around for a knife and when she had found it, attacked the pile of fresh loaves that lay at one end of the cutting board. She and Nat worked on in silence. Mrs. MacClaren came out once and got a basin of hot water. Mr. O'Connor came out once in a while and looked around helplessly.

Rose had platters piled high with bread when her mother came into the kitchen.

"Rose, run home and get the old linens that are in the hamper under the bed. Hurry now!" She disappeared into the bedroom again.

Rose, without coat or scarf, ran from the kitchen, closing the door carefully behind her. When she reached the cabin, she struggled with the wicker hamper for a few minutes and finally pried it open. She took out a pile of clean, worn linens and ran back to the cookhouse. Several shanty boys were standing at the door now.

"Gonna have a new river hog!" shouted Stove McCoy as Rose ran up.

"Guess so," said Rose, blushing. She pushed past them and closed the kitchen door after her as she entered.

122

Jake was at the stove now, lifting a huge kettle of potatoes from one of the burners.

"You're not going to cook now!" exclaimed Rose. He
turned in surprise.

"Your ma kicked me out. Guess there isn't much else
I can do. 'Cept wait," he added dolefully. He went on
more briskly, "Besides, Rosie, there's three million hungry loggers out there. It's my job to feed 'em, and that's
that."

Rose handed the linens to her mother, who had stuck
her head out of the bedroom door at that moment. Rose
continued helping, piling huge mounds of butter in
bowls. She helped Nat put butter and bread, baskets of
apples, plates of enormous cookies, salt, pepper, pots of
tea, jugs of milk, all up and down the long tables.

The kitchen door opened once and Stove's brown
head appeared. "What about it, Jake?" he said.

"Outta my kitchen!" yelled Jake, raising the meat hammer. Stove's head disappeared, but Rose could hear the laughter as the door closed behind him.

The steaks, pounded with flour and salt and cooked with water on top of the stove, were done. The potatoes were tender, the beans steaming.

Rose went out to ring the bell for Jake, and discovered that almost every man was standing or squatting silently outside the cookhouse.

"What news, Missy?" asked Bunker Jackson.

"Nothing yet," said Rose and gave the triangle that served as a bell a few good whacks with a rod. Men began filing in. There was something tense about their silence today, Rose decided, watching from the kitchen. They all looked at Jake as they entered and Rose realized they were almost as excited about the baby's coming as Jake was!

Before the men had started on the pies and cookies, a thin little cry sounded through the bedroom door. Jake dropped the spoon he held and rushed into the little room. Every sound along the tables stopped. Not a fork moved, cups were suspended in the air, bread half chewed. It seemed to Rose like centuries before Jake came out again.

"It's a boy!" he shouted. Cups clattered, forks banged down.

"Can we give 'im a cheer, Jake?" yelled a voice.

"Yes, but make it a small one. You know . . . ," he said and gestured to the bedroom.

There was a concerted cheer that shook the rafters.

"What's his name?" asked someone, but Jake had gone into the bedroom and there was no answer.

124

13 Battle

"No name," murmured a couple of the shanty boys, and then went back to their pie.

Rose had begun to help Nat and Jake clean up, when Jakie appeared, breathless in the kitchen door. His eyes were very red, but Rose decided to ignore that.

"How's Ma?" he asked, very low.

"She's fine. So's the baby," answered Rose.

When the loggers had gone, Rose, Nat and Jakie attacked the huge piles of dishes. Jake remained out of sight, still in the room with his wife and new son.

When Rose had put away the last cups, and Jakie had fed the scraps to the pig, they both put on their wraps and hurried outdoors. There was no sun in the grey sky and the muddy camp yard was dreary looking. In front of the bunkhouse, the washing-fire roared around a huge iron kettle. Francis Wilson had gone, but several men were busy stuffing socks and mittens into the kettle, and when it was full enough so that the surface of the water was broken by bumps and lumps, one of the men added a large can of liquid soap.

Army and Bunker stood by the kettle and poked at the contents with a stick. Rose noticed that they stood almost over their shoe tops in bright brown mud. Almost every vestige of snow in the camp had disappeared, and even the hard-packed, often-iced tote road looked mushy and showed bare earth along its sides.

When the last socks had been added, Army and Bunker began to talk, slowly and quietly. Rose could not hear what they were saying. Army seemed to grow more tense and began listing things on his fingers, waving them dangerously close under Bunker's nose. She still could not hear what they said. Finally, in answer to something Bunker said, Army's voice came through. "You're nuts!" he shrieked.

"Listen, you squirt!" Bunker shouted back, "I knew more about babies when I was three than you did your whole life!" Rose grinned at Jakie, but he didn't smile back.

"What's the matter?" asked Rose.

"They shouldn't oughta yell like that. Ma'll be sleepin'." Jakie looked fierce.

Army shrieked again and Bunker answered with more shouts. Nat came out the door behind Rose and Jakie.

"What's it all about?"

"Something about the baby," said Rose.

"I don't like it," said Nat.

"Yeah. They're gonna bother Ma."

"Not just that," said Nat, "but I heard Pa tell Mr. Borden that the men were edgy, not working and all. Some of them want whiskey. . . ." Rose gasped and

126

squeezed herself with both arms. Nat went on, "But Borden's real strict and he won't let 'em go into town and . . . and, well, a fight could start."

"Go get your pa," begged Jakie.

"I will, I will. I'm goin' now. You little kids back inside," he added. Rose nodded and moved swiftly toward the cookhouse door, but Jakie frowned and thrust out his lower lip and stayed where he was. Nat gave him a shove and then immediately set off at a trot toward the river, where Mr. MacClaren and Mr. Borden were at the rollways. Rose hoped prayerfully that they weren't too far away.

She peeked through a crack in the door. Army and Bunker were shouting and waving their arms.

"Listen! You listen! That baby ain't gonna have no girl's name!"

"You don't know nothin'!"

Both men shouted at once now and Rose couldn't make out what they were saying. A couple of idle loggers drifted over and soon the crowd was two deep around the arguing men. No one else had said anything until a voice called out, "He's right, Army. Keep your shirt on!"

Army whirled on the speaker and jabbed his finger in the man's chest.

"Keep outta this! You don't know nothin' either!"

A couple of voices from the crowd called out, "That's right! Keep your big mouth closed!" "Shut up, he kin talk if he wants to!" "What's it all about?"

Rose silently echoed this last call. Just at this moment the wagon pulled up in front of the blacksmith's shop and Francis Wilson jumped out and joined Jakie on the cookhouse stoop.

127

"What's it all about?" he asked Jakie, his voice rumbling steadily out of his huge chest.

"Don't know. Something about the baby," said Jakie in bewilderment.

"Mighta knowed. Anything to fight about. Army's been drinking, too. Borden'll kill him." Inside, Rose was shaking with fear now. "Where is Borden?"

"He and Rose's pa are at the river. Nat's gone to get 'em," Jakie answered.

"Looks bad." He stood a few minutes watching the shouting men. Then he strode to the group.

"Stop!" he roared. Every voice but Army Hughes' was still for a moment.

"Now, what's it all about?" asked Francis Wilson.

"Listen, Francis Wilson!" screamed Bunker. "You ever hear a *boy* baby named this? Named — listen, just listen — *Dagner?!*"

"Well-l-l . . ." rumbled the huge logger, while other voices took up the shouting. "I don't reckon I have." At this moment, Army picked up the small iron soap kettle and swung it at the back of Francis Wilson's head. The great figure slumped to the ground, silently.

"You dirty little. . . !" screamed Bunker, turning on Army.

"He had it comin'! He don't know nothin'!" This was accompanied by a shove. Someone tripped over the fire and sent it sputtering into the mud. In seconds it was trampled to lifelessness among stamping feet. Two fallers tackled a large swamper and the three rolled against the kettle of just lukewarm socks and sent it pouring sadly into the mud. In a second, Rose could no longer see the shape or color of the socks and mittens and in another second they were completely ground into the mud.

128

Rose was crying now and she called out to Jakie. "Is he all right? Is Francis Wilson all right?"

"No! He's out! He'll get hurt some more!" Rose plunged out the door.

"We've got to help him!" Tears were still pouring down her face.

"How can we? How can we?" shouted Jakie.

"We'll do it," muttered Rose and darted down the steps. Jakie called after her to stop, but then followed her almost immediately. They reached the still form of the man, and looking at his unconscious face, Rose realized how much she had grown to like him, how quiet and good his strength was. Around them the fight went

on; dollops of mud splashed Rose's dress, her hair, her face.

"Help me," she said fiercely to Jakie as she grabbed Francis Wilson's right arm. Jakie grabbed the other and they heard the man groan as they tugged. The slippery mud in which he lay helped them and finally, after pulling, tugging, resting and then going on, the two children managed to drag the unconscious man around the end of the cookhouse, and behind the pigpen.

"Blankets! Cloth! Water!" Rose spit these words at Jakie and the boy ran into the cookhouse. When he had gone, she reached under her dress and ripped the bottom of her petticoat and tugged until a piece came free. She used this to wipe the mud from Francis Wilson's face. Still he did not stir. Rose's tears dropped on his face.

The fight still raged in a knot around the now vanished washing fire. A small clot of men, rolling over and over each other in the mud, broke away from the main group, and soon another pair, squaring off with massive fists, took a stand near the blacksmith's shop, a couple of friends holding their coats and shouting insults at one another. The smith and his helper came out and in a few seconds they had tackled two drivers.

Army Hughes still stood in the middle of the yard screaming, "It ain't no girl's name! You don't know nothin' and you never have!"

From across the yard came the muffled voice of Bunker Jackson. "You ain't never heard it on no boy, you little weasel!" Two loaders were jumping on his back.

A swamper suddenly staggered out of the brawling mass still struggling where the fire had been, blood

130

streaming down the left side of his face. He sank to his knees and crawled to the pump outside the bunkhouse.

Rose cringed beside Jakie and the still silent form of Francis Wilson.

"Dagner! You low-down no-good louse! You stinkin' rat!" The shout came from the three mud-covered shanty boys pummeling a fourth near the bunkhouse.

Army was standing alone near the site of the washing now. The fight raged in front of the blacksmith shop, in the bunkhouse, on the fringes of the forest behind the barn. Jake had come out a few minutes before and with the two children had managed to drag Francis Wilson into the cookhouse, where he lay on the floor, Rose washing his face and Jakie covering him with blankets.

"Where's your pa, Rosie?" asked Jake.

"He's at the rollways. Nat's gone to get him."

"Hope he gets here soon. I gotta get back to Marian. Keep tryin', Rose. You're a good nurse." He patted her on the shoulder. "What's the fight about?" he asked.

"It's about the baby, I guess. What to name it."

Jake stood silently clenching his fists, then exploded a short loud laugh. "Them idiots!" he exclaimed and left to go in to see his wife.

Rose stepped to the door and looked across the clearing. The shanty boys she saw could barely be distinguished from the mud now. Piles of them were rolling and kicking at each other, covered with mire. Screams and bellows rang from inside the blacksmith shop. She saw chunks of wood thrown, and others hammered on stocking-capped heads. Army tackled a burly faller from behind and was kicked by another before he had touched the ground. Shouts and curses carried in the still, damp air.

131

Jake came out. "Well, at least it ain't so bad back there. They're keeping pretty much to the clearing." He shook his head as the form of Stove McCoy came hurtling through the air, in front of the kitchen window. He had been thrown by Frenchy Duke.

"You lousy . . . !" screamed Stove as he scrambled to his feet and ran after the peavy man.

The noise of battle filled the air when suddenly three sharp explosions rose above the din. A number of men stopped and looked around, then went back to their battling. Another sharp volley — this time Rose, who stood at the door, could see the wisps of smoke that followed — and more of the men stopped. Before they could begin again, Mr. Borden's voice could be heard shouting, "Stop it, the lot of you! Or I won't fire in the air next time!" Within seconds all the clearing was still, fists still poised, opponents sprawled in the mud, boots lowered quietly.

"Now I don't know what it's about and I don't give a curse!" His voice echoed in the silent clearing. "Settle down or I'll ship the lot o' ya'!" He stood with the pistol in his hand.

There were a few silent seconds and then shanty boys began picking themselves and their friends up from the mud.

Within a few minutes only Army and Bunker were left in the clearing. Without a word they had righted their laundry kettle and were scraping the mud from the clothes.

"Will it be all right now?" asked Rose in a whisper.

"Not really," answered Jake. "It's too quiet. They haven't forgotten . . . or they still feel like fighting, or something."

132

The kitchen was full of people, now. Nat and his father came in; Mrs. MacClaren softly closed the bedroom door as she entered the kitchen.

"You're coming home now, Rose," said her mother.

"Yes, Mother," said Rose, not moving. "Will he be all right?" She indicated the now stirring figure of Francis Wilson.

"We'll take care of him, Rosie," said Nathan. "We'll take him over to the bunkhouse and he'll be fine. See! He's coming around now." Francis Wilson groaned and slowly turned his head, without opening his eyes.

Reluctantly Rose pulled her shawl around herself and followed her mother back to the cabin.

When dinner time came, Mrs. MacClaren said, "I must go help Marian with the baby. And you'd better come along. Maybe you can help serve."

"But aren't you afraid to be there? For us, I mean?"

"Well, it can't be helped." She paused for several seconds. "I don't want you here alone. And Nat is right. He said they'll be calm until they eat." She paused again. "It's idleness, Rose. They need to work. If only it would snow, if only it would snow." Her voice trailed off in despair.

Nat met Rose with a whisper as she entered the cookhouse. "He's all right, Rose. He ate some food and he's sitting up. But don't tell Father or Mr. Borden I took food to him. If they can walk, they're supposed to be here."

Quiet as the cookhouse always was during meals, this evening it seemed more quiet than usual. Rose saw Army and Stove eyeing one another from opposite sides of the table. Lips were pressed together and fists lay clenched beside plates.

"It's gotta snow. And freeze. It's gotta," muttered Jake, as he stood behind Rose, watching the men.

"Yeah!" said Nat. It was almost a prayer.

Before the pumpkin pies and Indian pudding had disappeared, the door flung open and Mr. MacClaren rushed noisily in.

"Look at that, boys," he shouted and stepped aside so that the doorway was clear. A great swirl of snow followed him and then a chilling gust of wind.

There was a shout from the men and grins broke out around the table.

"Brrrrr!" said Rose, clasping her elbows.

"You may be cold, Rose," hollered Nathan, beating her on the back, "but it's back to work for the shanty boys!"

14 Drive

It snowed. And Rose thought it would never stop snowing. The morning after the fight, when she had gone to the barn for milk, she could hardly find her way there. The air had been peculiarly grayish white with blowing snow and the whole world seemed the same color. From that day on it had been deep winter. The drifts around the cabin seldom melted below the window sills.

Mr. MacClaren said, time and again, that it was a good winter for logging. Once the roads had been cleared, they stayed hard and useful with only the smallest amount of care. It didn't snow so often that they had to spend all their time plowing the roads, but the snow stayed deep all the time. When the paths were cleared, Rose could not see over the piles of snow on either side and plodded back and forth from the barn to the house to the chicken coop, hardly seeing a soul,

135

although all around on the sharp air were the sounds of the camp.

Mrs. MacClaren went often to the cookhouse, to help with the new baby, but after the big fight she had insisted that Rose stay out of the cookhouse, concentrate on schoolwork and housework, and play far less with Jakie. Remembering the fearful violence, neither Rose nor her father felt up to arguing the point. Nat had chilblains and so his mother insisted he stay in the cookhouse all day, only coming home to sleep. Often he didn't arrive until after Rose was in bed. She complained that it was like being in prison, and her mother, sighing, didn't contradict her.

Francis Wilson had recovered from the blow on the head Army had given him, although now and then he had bad headaches. He and Rose were friends now, and he was the only logger she ever saw during the closed-in weeks. He often came to the barn at milking time and helped her carry her one small pail of milk back to the cabin. Mrs. MacClaren smiled and thanked him at the door, but never invited him into the cabin.

"But he's my friend, Mother," protested Rose one evening.

"He's still a logger, Rose, and that's that."

"And so is Father!" Rose said with triumphant logic, "and they're both good and kind and. . . ."

"Your father is a scaler, Rose. A very high position!" Her mother spoke haughtily and turned back to the soup she was making.

Rose said with a toss of her head, "Well, when I'm grown up I'll invite him to *my* house."

Mildly her mother answered, "Don't be impertinent, Rose. Finish your bread."

136

And that was all she ever said to Rose on the subject of Francis Wilson, but Rose thought of him often and considered herself his true friend.

The winter crawled on. Icy snow, sleety snow, fluffy snow, heavy snow, light snow, driving, drifting, any kind Rose could imagine, fell and fell and fell. When the sun did shine, it seemed so terribly far away, utterly cold and brilliant, that Rose only felt colder.

March came and Rose expected to see wild flowers soon, but the snow lay undiminished around the trees and stumps and against the walls of the cabin. Rose noticed that the men were more in camp these days and she could hear the sounds of hammering and the clang of metal being worked. Her father said the logging was about done, the rollways were full, and soon the drive would start. Rose wondered when. When the river thawed, it seemed. Rose snorted and doubted that that would ever be.

At last, one morning, when she awoke and lay warmly huddled, she heard the sound of running water. Startled, she sat up and threw off the quilts. The slatted ventilator at the end of the attic showed her nothing. Dressing and scurrying down the ladder, she flung open the cabin door and the running-water sound seemed here to engulf the world. It was not a solid, constant roaring, as the river might make, but hundreds and thousands of small trickles, stopping and starting, now running ahead, now slowing. Just then an enormous clot of snow slid wetly from the cabin roof and landed to Rose's right. The snow lay squashed and grey under the eaves. Rose realized she could see the ground on the path that led to the barn. She smiled and drew in a breath of morning air. She stooped down and took a handful of snow. It was stiff and heavy and packed very tightly in her warm hand.

"It's thawing, it's thawing!" she sang.

And within a few days the snow had gone. It was that simple. Some still lay on the shaded sides of buildings and where it had drifted beneath the pines. Rose walked in the woods near the cabin, bare maple and beech branches rattling above her head. She found among the blackened leaves spring beauties and the new, sharp-rolled spears of skunk cabbage.

"Will the drive begin soon, Papa?" she asked her father one night.

"Not long now, Rosie." He seemed in good spirits these days.

"What do they do?"

"Well, they throw the sawlogs in the river and push 'em down to the mill," he answered jovially.

"Is it hard?" asked Rose.

"No," said Nat.

"Yes," said his mother.

They glared at each other for a few seconds.

"He'd like to be a river hog," explained Mr. Mac-Claren, "and she won't hear of it." He seemed to find this very funny.

"Oh, it's hard work," said Nat, "that's true, Ma, but I'm fast on my feet and that's more important." He seemed to be pleading now.

"I won't say I'll never let you, but not this year. You're too young, for one thing, to spend all those nights in camp outdoors with all those rough men."

"That's enough, son." Mr. MacClaren spoke seriously now. "Your mother's right. Maybe one of these years."

Nat looked depressed and rebellious.

138

"Going with Jake on the kitchen raft should be enough," said his mother in a comforting tone and Nat brightened slightly.

Rose knew nothing of the drive. The picture in her mind of the logs floating down to the towns and the mills was one of a gentle summer scene. How the men guided the logs she had no idea: bobbing along in boats, perhaps, or, where the river was narrowest, poking at them from the shore. Her mother's reaction to mention of the drive surprised her and made her uneasy. She hoped Nat would not disobey.

Finally, the call came.

"Drivin' pitch! Drivin' pitch!" echoed through the clearing.

"Drive begins tomorrow, Mame!" shouted her father, hurrying out of the cabin.

"Oh, goodness," she answered. "Rose, get out the two big kettles. We'll put the beans to soak now and cook them all night."

Later, as she and Rose sifted the white beans through their fingers into the water, Rose questioned her, "Why are we making so many beans?"

"There'll be lots of people we know, coming out from town, to see the drive." She swished her hand among the beans lying in the water. "It is kind of exciting, I'll admit."

"Will the Petersons be coming?"

"Oh, my, yes! At least, all but the baby, I guess."

"Will Emma come?"

"I expect."

Rose smiled with satisfaction. She had a plan and it needed Emma.

And Jakie. That afternoon, after she and her mother

had finally put the beans into crocks, where they swam in molasses, and set them in the fireplace oven, she asked to go and search him out. Mrs. MacClaren was preoccupied and absently nodded her permission. "For just a few minutes, though," she called after her daughter.

Jakie wasn't hard to find. He was at the blacksmith's shop, begging to work the bellows for Blackie.

"Jakie," called Rose softly. He turned. She beckoned to him. He frowned, but stepped away from the forge and out into the spring sunshine.

"Whatta ya' want?"

"This is the time," she said heavily. "We're going to get the man-catchers tomorrow. While everyone else is busy with the drive."

"No. I wanna watch the drive! Besides, just the two of us?"

"Oh, no, no, no! If that's what's worrying you! Heavens!" Rose laughed jovially.

"Well, who else?"

"Our friends the Petersons are coming out tomorrow."

"Oh." He still looked disgruntled and suspicious. And stubborn.

"Jakie, you can always see another drive, you know. But you can't always be in on the capture of criminals!" She stretched out the last word until it sounded heavy and ominous and huge.

Still he was silent.

Rose half turned. "We can't give you any credit for the capture if you're not there," she said and began, very slowly, to turn away.

"Well," said Jakie, "I guess. . . ."

"Good!" said Rose. "I'll meet you at the rollways tomorrow morning and we'll plan some more then."

140

In the distance, she could hear her mother calling her.
"I'll see you tomorrow then," she repeated.

"All right!" said Jakie, his thoughts returning to the
smithy.

All day Rose and her mother had cooked and baked.
By evening Rose was so exhausted she could hardly lift
the pail as she started home from the barn with the milk.
She sighed mightily and then a voice spoke behind her,
" 'Lo, Miss Rose." A huge, brown paw took the pail from
her weary hand.

"Oh, Francis Wilson! I'm so glad to see you! Thank
you for carrying the pail. I'm so tired," she babbled
on, "we've been cooking food for a regular army all
day. . . ."

"Oh, sure," he interrupted quietly. "For the start of
the drive." He didn't seem any happier about it than
her mother did. She'd grumbled at Rose all day about
"curiosity seekers."

"What's so wrong with it, Francis Wilson? Tell me."

"Oh, there's nothing wrong with it, I reckon. But,
well, there's times when I think they just come a hopin'
some poor shanty boy'll be killed."

"Oh!" Rose didn't know what to say. She was shocked.
No one had told her the danger was that real. Certainly
not from just putting a few logs in the river. They
walked on a few paces.

"What do you do on the drive, Francis Wilson?" said
Rose, changing the subject, she hoped.

"Oh," he laughed, "I'm just a river hog! None o' that
dangerous stuff of breakin' out the rollways for me!
Give me a good solid sawlog under my caulks!" Rose
didn't completely understand, but before she could ask

141

him questions, questions she knew he'd take the time to answer, if no one else would, they had come to the cabin door and Rose's mother, worn and draggled looking, stood on the stoop to greet them.

"Evenin', Miz MacClaren," said Francis Wilson and tipped his hat.

"Hello, Francis Wilson, and thank you for carrying Rose's pail." She smiled wanly and waved Rose into the cabin.

" 'Bye, Francis Wilson. I'll watch for you tomorrow."

" 'Night, Miss Rose," and he was gone.

The next day was cloudy at dawn, but cleared before the breakfast dishes had been washed, and Rose knew a growing excitement as her mother banked the fire under the last of the beans and tied on a straw bonnet, preparing to leave the house.

Rose ran up to the attic to get her shawl. She started violently as she saw Nat standing outside the curtain that separated their rooms.

"Oh! You gave me a fright! I thought you were gone. What are you doing?" This last she asked as she realized he was bent almost double tearing at the legs of his trousers.

"Sawin' off my britches, that's what!" he said angrily, panting and gritting his teeth as the hard, coarse material resisted his efforts.

Rose giggled.

"Let me do it. I'll get my scissors." She disappeared into her half of the attic and came back a moment later with a pair of scissors shaped like a large-eyed stork. She bent down and started cutting Nat's trousers off below the knee.

142

"It won't look right. I should do it with a knife," he muttered.

"All right," and Rose sighed in an exaggerated fashion. "I'll cut it jaggedly." And she did. She finished efficiently in a few seconds and Nat looked down at the results. The bottoms of the now short legs were jaggedy all right, and he looked grudgingly pleased.

"Thanks," he growled.

"But why did you do it? Mother will be furious."

" 'Cause you can't work on the drive with long pants, silly!"

"Oh." Then a thought occurred to Rose. "You aren't going to disobey Mama and be — what do you call it? — a river hog?"

"Don't worry," he said, and clattered down the ladder ahead of her.

Rose shrugged her shoulders and followed. Nat had ducked out of the door before his mother could see him. She was putting on her bonnet at the mirror behind the fireplace.

"Let's be on our way, Rose. And stay with me at all times."

They walked the tote road as far as the river. A little way ahead was Mrs. O'Connor, carrying a large basket that Rose knew held the baby. Jakie ran alongside, now ahead, now falling back to say things to his mother and then to run ahead again. Rose walked sedately beside Mrs. MacClaren. The mud was sticky, but the sides of the road were worse.

When they reached the river, they stopped a moment and Rose looked up and down the banks. In places there were still hardwood stands, back away from the banks, and she could see that these little spots of woods were

143

filled with women and children. In the vast places where
the pine had been cut, men and boys perched, sat, and
stood on the stumps. The sun was warm and already
they were taking off their jackets and wiping their fore-
heads with large red or blue handkerchiefs. Mrs. Mac-
Claren pulled Rose toward the nearest group of women.
They were standing under a closely set group of maples,
just barely budding with the orange and green of new
leaves. The ground here was firmer and not as muddy
as the churned-up road and the paths near the river.
Rose settled her shoulder against a tree and looked
around.

At the river bank itself, behind the rollways, dozens
of men were milling. Most of the loggers Rose knew,
but there were a few new faces too, and since they were
new faces, they looked hard and cold to Rose.

"Rose? H'lo," said a voice at her shoulder.

She turned and looked into the blue eyes of Emma
Peterson.

"Emma! You've come!" Rose smiled broadly and
grabbed Emma's arm. "Emma, I have a plan. We'll talk
about it later. At dinner, maybe. You and me and Jakie
have something important to do." Her voice was low
and urgent. Emma was obviously delighted with the re-
ception Rose had given her and blushed with pleasure
without really hearing her last words.

"Why're you here, Emma?" Rose thought of the
things Francis Wilson had told her.

"Oh, Papa works for the boom company at drive
time." Her voice was stronger and more confident now.

"The . . . boom company?"

"Yes." Emma frowned. "Doesn't anybody tell you
anythin'?"

144

"That's about it," sighed Rose.

"Well, the boom company takes charge of all the logs, once the drive has started. Look, there he is.'

Rose looked where Emma pointed and saw Mr. Peterson, dressed in a black suit and a derby hat, driving a wagon. He was halted now, talking down to a gaily dressed logger who held a peavy. There was a bright red scarf around the logger's waist and Rose could see that his pants had been cut off just below the knee, like Nat's, and stuffed into boots that had vicious-looking spikes on their soles. Rose could see the bottom of one of his boots where he had propped it up on a wagon wheel.

"Papa's tellin' 'em when to start. That's part of his job," said Emma with a smirk. "It'll be any minute now."

"What do they do?" asked Rose, rather frantically. She was afraid she would miss the start of the drive and never know it.

"Just watch, you'll see," answered Emma.

Rose watched intently. The rollways were ahead of her, the logs piled precariously along the river banks. Rose couldn't see the river, so high were the piles of logs. In fact, it was a long, long wall between her and the river. Logs were all she could see, as far as she looked, and she knew the other side of the river was the same way.

A hush fell over the crowds of women in the maple grove, the men and boys standing among the pine stumps, the loggers wandering back and forth behind the rollways.

Mr. Peterson finished talking to the logger and drove away in the wagon toward the upstream camps. Everyone turned to watch the logger as he moved toward the nearest part of the rollways. The sun shone warmly and blue jays called importantly as the logger, Buck, approached the wall of logs. It was like church, thought Rose, like waiting for the preacher to open his Bible and put on his spectacles. Buck was dignified and looked at the pile as a judge would look, weighing in his mind every log. Tentatively, he struck his peavy in the end of a log near the bottom; a stir rustled the crowd, very faintly. But Buck changed his mind and, more firmly now, pushed the peavy into a nearby log. He wiped his face with his handkerchief.

"The key log," whispered Emma, very closely into Rose's ear.

Looking around with a very theatrical gaze, Buck bent to his work and, with a mighty heave, pulled the log out

of the pile. It looked to Rose as if he flung the log into the river, but she had hardly time to see because a hollow rumbling had begun and slowly at first, but faster and faster, the enormous pile of logs was falling into the river! Buck jumped aside with a businesslike glance at the falling logs, some still coated with ice and snow. "Go to town with it, boys!" he shouted, and turned to the next rollway. The crowd cheered and hollered and whistled as he demonstrated his skill time after time in the next hour or two. Once or twice he gave the crowd a thrill as he almost got caught himself in the avalanche of logs.

"Not getting caught is what makes him great," said Jakie, who had joined Emma and Rose.

In a while the activity right in front of them had died down and Rose ventured onto the river-bank path. She looked down into the water, not far below at this point. She gasped.

The river looked as if it were made of wood. From shore to shore the logs headed downstream, only now and then did a glance of sparkling water show how they were moving. Here and there were men standing, feet apart, knees slightly bent, riding on logs, their long cant hooks or peavies held chest high at the ready. Rose thought they looked like knights with their lances held for a tournament.

The sight was breathtaking for the girl from the quiet Eastern farm. The sun, the breeze, the rubbing, crashing, thumping of the log-covered river, and down the banks the still-falling piles of logs and the shouts of the watchers.

"How wonderful! I never . . . never thought it would be like *this*."

147

"This ain't nothin'," said Jakie. "Wait'll the winter's cut is in, in a day or two, why, you wouldn't even believe the river could hold it all." Jakie tried to sound careless about it all. But Rose could tell that he, too, was excited. She said nothing for a moment but stood still, listening and watching.

"Where's Francis Wilson," she asked finally.

"He's up ahead with the jam crew," answered Jakie.

"What's that?" asked Rose.

"Them's the river hogs that watches for log jams — you know, if they don't float along each, like they should, but get caught on somethin', or each other, and stop up the whole stream. Anyway, only the best men get to be in the jam crew o' course."

"Your ma'll be taking us up to town tomorrow and you kin see the place where the drive ends then," volunteered Emma.

"Ends?" murmured Rose. "How can it ever end? It's too wonderful to end."

The sunny river heaved below her, bearing on its back the logs that would build the railroads, the towns, the cities of the nation, and then, incredibly, Army Hughes rode by, balancing on his log like a dancer. He waved his cant hook at the children standing above.

15 Capture

At noon Rose and Emma helped their mothers, and Mrs. O'Connor put out huge loaves of bread to go with the beans, and enormous pots of coffee. Others who came to watch the drive brought pies and cakes and potato salads and hams.

During the meal, Rose and Emma and Jakie waited impatiently until they could be alone to talk about their plans. Emma was nervous, but Jakie was now as excited as Rose, and as eager to get on with their project.

The dinner was served in the clearing, away from the breeze of the river, and away from its roar and crash. It was hot in the clearing, and after the meal the three children stood wearily under a tree waiting to help pick up dishes.

"Where's your papa, Jakie? Why'd your ma do everything?"

"Don't you know anything, Rose?" sneered Jakie. "He's. . . ."

149

"Why should I know anything?" flared Rose, interrupting him. "Nobody ever, *ever* tells me anything!" She was hot and tired and impatient.

Jakie looked astonished and Emma smug. After a moment's silence, Jakie went on. "Well, he's on the wanigan and. . . ."

"The what?" asked Rose.

"The wanigan." Jakie was careful not to sneer. "It's a kind of raft and it follows the logs down the river. My pa cooks the meals on her and takes 'em ashore to feed the men. And they carry extra socks and cant hooks and peavies and things like that."

"Oh. Yes," she added with sudden inspiration, "that's what Nat's doing, too, isn't it?"

"Yeah," agreed Jakie.

Their mothers beckoned to them just then, and for a little while they picked up dishes, stacked platters, bundled cups and spoons and forks into huge dish pans where other boys and girls were washing and drying dishes. It didn't take long and soon the clearing was quiet, mothers and babies and toddlers stretched in the shade at the edge of the clearing for naps, old men and women gossiping quietly in the spring sunshine. Rose and Emma and Jakie slipped away.

Their feet found the muddy road a little drier and harder now. Hours before they had discarded their shoes and stockings, although Rose's mother had frowned.

"We've got to go downriver," said Rose importantly, as they trotted toward the river. The roar came through the trees to meet them, singing now with the clatter and crash of the logs it held.

When they reached the banks the roar was like a wall. The friends stood for a moment looking down, a sunny wind whipping their hair and their clothes. After the prisonlike winter, Rose felt like a ball that had been held in the bottom of a pail of water, and now she'd been released and she might possibly fly into the sky with the joy of her freedom.

As far as they could see, on either hand, the river was full, a mass of logs from bank to bank, so full that logs still hung on the banks below the rollways, as if there were no room for them below.

For a few minutes they stood hypnotized by the sight. A clear stretch of water appeared, between masses of logs.

"Look!" exclaimed Rose.

"Yep, it's the wanigan," replied Jakie.

None of them said anything more for several minutes. Slowly, as if it were crawling, the wanigan moved downstream, close to the bank opposite.

Rose looked for Nat, peering through the sparkles thrown into her eyes by the water. Only Jake appeared, standing beside a low structure at one side of the raft. He was bending over something on the deck. He didn't see their waves.

"What . . . what are we going to do, Rose?" ventured Emma at last.

"What? Oh! Yes!" said Rose, as if awakening from sleep. "Our plans! Well, we're going to catch the man-catchers who took Nat, that's what we're going to do!" She began moving down the path beside the river.

Emma gasped and did not follow for a moment.

"How, Rose? How?" she asked breathlessly.

"Well, you remember, Jakie," she answered, appealing to his sullen face, "how that man, the one who played the fiddle, said he'd seen one of them. . . ."

151

"You only think it's one of 'em. . . ."

"Oh, it is all right. I know!"

"But how . . . ?" asked Emma, trotting now beside the other two.

"We'll think of something when we find them," muttered Rose.

Jakie laughed. "I guess the three of us oughta be able to tie him up!"

Rose glanced again at the river and stopped suddenly.

"Look! Look, it's him! I know it is." Alone, riding a log, was a single man, his beard glinting in the sun.

"You're right, Rose! What'll we do?" Jakie's question was urgent.

Without hesitating, Rose began to retrace her steps to the camp. "Help! Help!" she called as she ran. Emma and Jakie followed.

It seemed to take forever to reach the clearing. Only a couple of women were visible.

"Help! It's the man-catcher! He's on the river! It's him, it's him! Come quick!" she cried as she clutched the sleeve of one of the women. The woman, whom Rose did not know, turned in consternation.

"Calm yourself, child. What do you want?"

"I want you to catch him. Where are the men? Where's my father? Help!" She was running frantically around now, but the two women just stared at her. An old man got up from his nap under the trees and stood leaning on a cane, staring also.

"You'll have to wait, child. They're all gone. Now calm yourself."

"Where's my mother?"

"Miz MacClaren, ain't it? Why, she's . . . I ain't sure."

"Mother! Mother!" called Rose. She stopped running

152

and turned to Emma and Jakie running toward her.

"There's no one to do anything! We'll have to do it ourselves. Let's go!"

Emma and Jakie followed her wearily.

"Come on, come on!" They all ran faster. Far behind them now they could hear the women calling, "Where you off to? What's wrong? Wait, wait . . . !" But they were gone.

They reached the river and turned onto the path going downriver. On they ran, Emma slipping now and then in the muddy path. They came eventually to the small stream that marked the place where Rose, following her father and Francis Wilson so many weeks ago, had gone toward the deserted camp. She stopped.

Above the insistent roar of the river she shouted, "I think," and then fearful of being heard by someone else, lowered her voice, finding it possible to talk under the sound, somehow, "I think we should turn off here and go look at the camp."

"No," said Jakie vehemently. "No! They wouldn't stay around there! It was up where the next stream comes into the river that he saw him." He started running again and Rose, feeling that things were out of her control, followed as he and Emma leaped across the little stream. She landed on the other side in mud that squished between her bare toes.

It was not long before they reached the banks of the next stream. It was somewhat larger than the other tributary, but still not large enough to serve as a carrier of logs, and it was very shallow where the road crossed it. The three stopped at a motion of Jakie's hand and stood listening and looking for a moment. They could hear only the roar of the river, but through the sapling

153

maples and knee-high pine seedlings Rose saw a flash of metal near the river's edge.

"Down," she whispered, pulling Emma and Jakie into the shelter of the undergrowth. She pointed out what she had seen. The others saw it too.

"Let's creep up there and see what's going on," she said.

Slowly, as silently as possible, they moved toward the river. Shortly Rose could see the river, the logs, and, standing on the banks, the red-bearded man, a long pike pole in one hand and a cant hook in the other. Silently she pointed him out to the other two. Squatting uncomfortably in the bushes, they watched him for a few minutes. The man, who looked as thin and ragged as he had when the fiddler had seen him at Christmas time, reached suddenly into the stream with the pike pole and levered a sizable log toward the shore, grabbing it with the cant hook when it floated close and pulling it onto the bank, which was low at this point where the stream entered the river.

"He's robbin' the stream!" Jakie muttered urgently to the girls.

"Oh, dear," sobbed Emma.

"Shhh," said Rose.

"A log pirate!" said Jakie heavily.

By stretching her neck, Rose could see now that there was a pretty big pile of logs resting half hidden in the underbrush back of the man. He struggled to add the newest log to the pile. The children watched for a few more seconds, then Rose moved away from the river, silently, pulling the others after her, to the underbrush on the other side of the stream. They crouched together again.

154

"Tell me quickly about it, Jakie."

Jakie understood. "Well, he'll saw off the brand that's on 'em and put his own on and toss 'em back in the river, and when they get to Bay City, he'll be there to claim 'em and get the money for 'em. He won't get many, alone like that, but he'll get beer money. . . ."

Emma and Rose exchanged glances.

". . . and maybe enough to ship out quick, before he's arrested. For man-catching."

"That'd be foolish! He must know one of us would recognize him. He must know Nat's still around and we'd know him!"

"He'd shave," said Emma softly.

"What?" asked Rose and Jakie together.

"He'd shave, o' course. We wouldn't know him without that red beard, now, would we?"

"You're right! Thank you, Emma. So, that means we've got to do something now."

"And quick, 'cause it'll be dark 'fore too long."

It was true, they'd come a long way and morning seemed years back to Rose. The afternoon sun was lowering and through the trees they could see the banks casting long shadows on the full and clashing river.

"Can we tie him up, Jakie?"

"Oh, Rose, with that cant hook in his hand!" exclaimed Emma.

"Yeah, and that pike pole."

They sat quietly a moment.

"He must have a camp around here someplace," said Rose, "let's find it."

She stood up and the others followed as she stepped gingerly through the underbrush, her bare feet fearful of sharp sticks and slimy leaves. She followed the little

155

stream for a while and finally reached a very small clearing on the banks. A rough lean-to stood at one side and a stone-circle fireplace in the center. The ground was scuffed and bare and a litter of kettles, wood chips, and a few tools lay around. A single stump with a box beside it seemed to have served as a table. The camp was a poor one and Rose felt herself fighting down pity for the man who had lived here through such a hard winter.

"Ain't much of a camp!" sneered Jakie.

"What now?" asked Emma.

"Shhh!" said Rose urgently. They listened and heard the crash of heavy boots plodding through the underbrush toward the camp.

Emma gasped.

"Quick, across the stream!" The other two followed Rose as she splashed noisily across and into the underbrush on the far side. The three flopped to their stomachs and lay without breathing or looking.

Gone now were ideas of capturing the man by themselves. The thought of confronting him at all made them hot and frightened in the pits of their stomachs. Escape was all the hope that occupied their minds now.

"Wha's that?" they heard their pursuer mutter. The boots rang more quickly and the three on the other side of the stream seemed to bury themselves in the wet leaves, twigs, vines, and branches among which they lay.

"Just a 'coon, I reckon," he muttered loudly.

After a while, they raised their heads and watched the afternoon slip away as the red-bearded man built a small fire, put on a kettle of water, brewed himself some coffee, and sat drinking it at his small table. He looked at the sky from time to time; meanwhile he had some

156

bread and meat of some kind. Jakie's stomach growled and Rose poked him.

At last, when twilight had filled the sky with lavender and rose, he reached inside the lean-to and produced a saw. Jakie snorted softly and nodded his head. The man set off again for the river bank, plodding through the underbrush. In a moment he was out of sight.

Rose gasped, Emma groaned, and Jakie stretched. Muttering, they rose slowly to their feet, their bodies aching. Their ankles were red with the marks of the sticks on which they had lain, their elbows and knees were damp from leaf mold. Emma had a smear of dirt across her forehead and on Rose's left cheek was the pattern of an ancient maple leaf on which she had lain for so long.

"Let's go," said Jakie, taking charge. He ran for the middle of the stream. Carefully and quite silently he ran through the water in the direction of the river. The girls followed.

When they reached the river-bank road, they stopped. The river was dark now, between its high banks.

"Which way, which way?" asked Rose.

"Not back to camp. It's more'n a mile and a half back. There's a fly boom along a ways. We'll go toward town."

"My mother . . . ," began Emma.

"And mine," said Rose matter-of-factly.

"It can't be helped," said Jakie, "it's almost dark. There'll be a camp at the fly boom and we can get someone there to help us."

This revived memories of the courageous plan and Rose's spirits sagged, remembering how panicked they had been at the man's camp. She followed Jakie docilely as he started down the road, away from camp and home.

157

They left the small stream where the road crossed it and set off together, silently. As they traveled, her anger at herself grew and grew. At last she stopped suddenly.

"I won't go back! Not without that . . . that man-catcher!"

Emma looked frightened.

Jakie asked, "Well, what d'ya think you can do?"

"We'll . . . we'll attack him! And hit him with a log and tie him to a tree and . . . and then we'll go get some-one. Come on!"

Without waiting to hear their answers, Rose pulled Emma and Jakie after her as she turned in the path and started back toward the man-catcher. She was back at the little stream in a few minutes and, pausing only a moment, waded quietly through. She motioned the others to be quiet also, and she got to her hands and knees to push through the broken underbrush toward the red-bearded man's station on the river. Almost there, she paused and signaled the others to do so, too. Only the roar of the river was to be heard and a few birds saying good night. Rose stuck her head up above the under-brush and looked carefully around. For a second she saw nothing and then her eyes fell on a figure stretched beneath a tree. She stood straight up and heard Emma and Jakie gasp behind her. She stepped boldly but slowly into the open. One step at a time she approached the tree, feeling that even the river's sound could not hide her footsteps.

The figure under the tree did not move.

Closer and closer she stepped. She could hear a snor-ing now, almost as loud as the river. Finally, the man was in full view, lying stretched on the ground, sound asleep. Six or seven huge logs were lying by the river-

158

side. Rose supposed he was exhausted from his work. Silently she motioned Jakie and Emma from the bushes. They approached very quietly.

"Dead drunk," whispered Jakie.

"How do you know?"

"Just a guess," Jakie whispered.

"Where's some rope?" asked Rose in an undertone, while Emma shivered beside her.

For a few minutes they stood looking around them, anxious and frustrated.

"My belt!" said Jakie with sudden inspiration and, taking it off, handed it to Rose. It was a length of hemp rope raveled at the ends and softly pliable, but still strong and unworn.

"Our aprons, Rose," said Emma, "rolled up, maybe?" Rose nodded her approval and she and Emma fashioned thick ropes from their aprons.

"Oh, look!" Rose whispered excitedly. It wasn't rope she saw, but three or four feet of heavy coarse webbing straps, damp from the river.

"Probably used it to haul in the logs, once he snagged 'em."

Rose thought this was time for careful planning. She beckoned the other two back into the bushes.

"What do you think, Jakie?" she asked.

"I don't know. Tie his hands and feet, I guess, and run like fury for help."

"Hmmm. Emma?"

"Whatever you say, Rose."

She thought for several minutes, looking around the river bank as she crouched.

"Like this, maybe. His hands are lying at his sides. Emma, you take one, Jakie the other. I'll do his feet.

159

Now, listen, this is how we'll do it. You tie the rope to his hand, Emma, then run quickly with the other end to that little tree there and tie it around the tree quick. Jakie, you do the same with the other arm, tying it out straight to that other tree over there. I'll tie his feet together with one of the straps and then pull them out straight to that one log that's kind of leaning over, under all the rest. Now, we've gotta act together, at just the same time, and *fast!*"

"What if . . . what if . . . something goes wrong?" Emma could hardly speak.

"Then we'll all get caught and thrown in the river," said Rose, a bit of exasperation in her voice.

Emma whimpered, but took the rope Rose held out and found the ends.

Out of the brush they crept. The man slept on, his breathing heavy. Quietly, cautiously, slowly, each of the group maneuvered a rope or strap or apron around the man's limbs. He twitched and groaned, but moved very little, and slept on. Finally, all the preliminary tying had been done. Now was the dangerous time. Each capturer stretched his rope around the thing to which he would fasten the arm or legs without pulling it tight. When they were all set, Rose called.

"Now!" The bindings were yanked tightly around the trees and the logs and fumbling hands began tying.

"*Whaaaaaaa????!!!!*" roared the groggy, suddenly awakened captive.

"Good and tight!" screamed Rose, winding the strap about itself as she finished her knot.

The three stood looking down at the captive.

A string of curses came from his lips.

"It's not quite tight enough," said Rose calmly. "He

160

mustn't thrash around so." She looked around. A hatchet lay beside the logs. "I know, we'll stake him down across the middle, too." With another strap and the points of the cant hook and pike pole through the ends, she strapped the logger down around and across his stomach.

"Now, run, Jakie, run downstream and get help!"

16 REward

Emma was crying, a kind of moaning wail.

"Emma, dear," said Rose crossly, "it's all right, can't you see that? Jakie will be back soon with help."

"*Noooooooooo, he won't.*"

"Shut up, girlie," said the red-bearded logger lying staked to the ground. He sounded weary and a little weak.

Emma stopped instantly and looked at the man.

"Whadda ya' want to do this to me, a harmless ol' man, fer?"

Rose's mouth hardened.

"Don't answer him, Emma," she said, as the other girl opened her mouth.

"What's the matter, you girl, you've got me fair and square. Couldn't you at least undo my hand so I could smoke my pipe?"

"What do you think, Rose?" whispered Emma.

"Yore paw likes a pipe, now and again in a tight spot, I reckon," he pleaded.

Emma looked panicky.

"He's not your papa, Emma! For goodness' sake! He's a criminal! A man-catcher! We don't have to do what he says!" With each word she spoke, Rose's voice grew stronger and more confident.

The logger snarled wordlessly and struggled for a few minutes with his bonds.

Rose walked to him and, looking full in his face, said sternly, "Stop it! Or I'll have to sit on *your* head!"

The man stopped instantly. "So *you're* the one! Pore ol' Billito told me you 'bout squashed out his brains." He laughed sadly.

Rose picked up a short, heavy piece of wood and shook it threateningly at the man. She stooped to find another and thrust it into Emma's hand. Then she picked up what at first appeared to be just a smooth, short piece of wood, but was a mallet of some kind. She looked and gave a cry.

"Look! Emma, look! It's a branding hammer. Like my papa uses! Only this's got a different sign on it!" She ran to the pile of logs to which the captive's feet were tied. She looked at the ends of the logs and the ground around them. She picked up a circular piece of wood, bigger than her mother's turkey platter, and examined it.

"Oh, Emma, look!" she said in a horrified voice. "He's already cut off the brand my papa made and put on his own." Both girls looked at the logger with scandalized eyes. They stood accusingly beside him for a moment. His face was dark and closed, his mouth unreadable behind his beard.

"C'mon, Emma. Let's sit down."

164

They sat on a stump not far from their captive, Emma shivering and Rose looking fierce and stern.

"I wish they'd come," whispered Emma.

Rose did too. Back down the river, around the bend toward Duck Tree Camp — home — the sun had just about set. The river was quieter for a moment. No logs rode its back for a short space. The rich pink of the sunset filled the river's waters. It felt lonely to Rose. She shivered, too, once.

The pink on the river died and the water turned a faded grey.

Finally, far off, it seemed, they heard shouts. They both stood and looked expectantly along the path through the woods across the little stream. The man on the ground began thrashing again, but stopped when Rose menaced him with her club.

In a few minutes the sounds were unmistakable and suddenly there emerged from the gloom into the dying daylight beside the river Jakie, running and shouting, leading her father, Emma's father, Army, and Francis Wilson.

The captive began shouting, too. Emma wailed. The rest of the men hollered and called to one another. Rose and her father clung to each other for a moment, and Rose began to cry.

In a few complicated minutes the men had untied the logger, hoisted him to his feet, tied his hands securely behind his back, and began to march him back the way they had come. Mr. Peterson led the way. Rose's father and Francis Wilson followed with the red-bearded man-catcher between them. Rose, Emma and Jakie were next, with Army bringing up the rear.

As they all moved quickly through the darkening

woods — Rose could just barely see Emma's father at the head of the cavalcade, the three captors shouted breathlessly at one another.

". . . didn't think I'd ever find the fly boom . . . !"

"Oooooooo, he was gonna get us, Rose . . . !"

". . . you'd *never* come. . . ."

After a few minutes of trotting through the woods, they fell silent. Rose watched the three ahead of her. The man looked dwarfed and shaken between her father and Francis Wilson. He stumbled and the men on either side grabbed his arms above the elbow. They kept their hold on him until the group finally reached the camp, which was at one side of the fly boom. Another animal, thought Rose suddenly. Jakie explained, "It's a place part way along the river where they've rigged up this boom. It'll stop the whole drive dead in its tracks, if there should be a jam ahead that needs untanglin'."

Emma and Rose looked around the makeshift camp timidly.

"Look what we got, boys!" shouted Army.

"And there's the little gals what did it," added Francis Wilson, flinging a huge arm in the direction of the girls.

There was a shout and a cheer from the handful of shanty boys who sat around a campfire in the center of a small clearing beside the river. They were sitting on stumps or the ground or decaying logs.

The shanty boys argued for a while about what to do with the captive.

"String him up," stated one.

"Take him into town. Toss him in the hoosegow."

"String him up!"

"There's a reeward for him, you reckon?"

"String him up!"

166

"He's goin' into town, boys," broke in Francis Wilson. "And tonight. I don't want the keepin' of him overnight. He's skinny enough, for sure, but still crafty, I betcha. And there won't be no lynchin'," he finished.

Rose was thankful and relieved. She had been a strong and resourceful hunter when she had gone after her quarry, but now, with her father there, and Francis Wilson, her knees were weak and she felt her jaw quivering, as Emma's had been all evening.

"Come, Rose," said her father, "and you, too, Emma and Jakie." He led them to the fire, and made them sit side by side on a log there. Then he handed each a tin plate and a spoon. From a huge kettle sitting beside the fire, he ladled stew into their plates. Then he cut off a hunk of bread for each and said, "Eat first. Then we'll talk." Rose caught the menace in his voice, but was suddenly too hungry to care.

She watched Francis Wilson and one of the other shanty boys light lanterns and set off through the woods with their captive. She finished her meal and her eyes began to sag.

"Before you go to sleep, Miss, I want a word with you." It was her father.

She followed him to the edge of the circle of firelight and stood before him with a smile.

"No need to smile, Rose. You've done a dangerous and foolhardy thing."

"But, Papa. . . ."

"I know, I know. You captured the man who kidnapped Nat."

"And was stealing wood from the drive!"

She darted suddenly back to the log on which she had been sitting and snatched up the branding axe she had **found.**

167

"Look, Papa! Look!"

Her father took the tool from her and looked at it without surprise, but with some pleasure, Rose felt.

"Hmmm. Oh, this is a good find. So was capturing the man, but, Rose, no one knew where you were. Your mother was sick with worry. She'll suffer now until Francis Wilson gets to Bay City — which is where she is now — and tells her you're all right."

Rose hung her head.

"We tried to tell them. We tried."

"We know that now. In fact, in a few minutes after you saw him we'd started out to hunt for him." He paused and again examined the branding axe. "We just never thought he'd get off the river so soon, I guess. Anyway, we missed the spot where you found him." He paused again. "And remember you're a girl, Rose. And I hope you'll be a lady."

Suddenly Rose was very angry. She tightened her lips till they turned white. She scraped her toes through the dirt of the clearing. Her father patted her on the shoulder, smiled benignly, and finished, "I won't punish you this time. But try and behave in the future."

He walked away.

"I'll never be a lady," she muttered. Emma joined her then.

"Did he scold you good? You gonna get a lickin'?" Emma smoothed her skirt carefully. "I am. Soon's we get to town tomorrow." Rose thought she seemed almost happy.

"No lickin'. You'd think being a girl meant I didn't have any brains," she snarled at the startled Emma. "Or courage. Or anything. I won't be a lady. Never." She flounced off toward the fire and sat looking ominous on a stump next to Jakie.

168

Her anger had wakened her completely and so banished her weariness that when her father came and told the two girls they should take blankets and sleep in the low tent that held supplies, she felt she was hardly ready for bed. Emma dragged her toward the tent and they crawled inside together.

"Our pas'll sleep right outside."

"I'm not afraid."

"Rose, you're never afraid of anything. You're as good as a boy." Emma snuggled sleepily into her blanket and was asleep almost instantly.

"You bet I am," murmured Rose.

Morning dawned with a grey misty drizzle over the river and the camp. Breakfast was cornmeal mush, watery from the rain and burned from the fire. Rose and Emma and Jakie finished eating and Mr. MacClaren and Mr. Peterson prepared to take them into Bay City. Mr. Peterson's horse and small buggy were just outside the camp and by the time the three had eaten, the horse was hitched up and the five could be on their way.

The long ride was uncomfortable. The youngsters, shoeless and wearing only the clothes they had worn the day before, which had been a warmer, sunny, spring day, were chilled by the rain. And the nearer Bay City the buggy came, the more apprehensive Rose became. She had been thinking about her mother all morning and wondering what she would say and do. She wiggled nervously. Emma was calmer now, now that they were approaching her own home. She's so sure, Rose thought, she knows she's been bad and deserves her punishment. So she can be quite calm and happy.

"I wish I knew," she muttered.

"What did you say, Rose?"

"Nothing. Nothing at all."

"You afraid of your ma, too? I didn't think you were ever afraid," Emma said.

"Yeah, you're always talkin' about courage," said Jakie.

"Oh, I can be scared too."

"Well, I reckon she'll be so glad to see you she won't hardly say nothin'. You wait and see," Jakie said.

"That's right," agreed Emma.

"Have you done this before?" asked Rose, puzzled.

"Not this, preeecisely," said Emma complacently, "but once my brother run off, 'most to Chicago. . . ."

Rose looked interested.

". . . 'n when he come home it was like Jakie said."

"I've done it too," said Jakie.

The three fell silent, Emma calm and confident now, Rose nervous and shaky, Jakie resigned and quiet.

Pretty soon, through the misting drizzle, they could see the town lying ahead, low along the river banks, the smoke from the sawmills rising straight into the sky. Soon the road left the river bank, and passed through the drab outskirts of the town. At the noise of the buggy wheels, ragged children came to stand in the doorways of the stark cabins, often their mothers or fathers behind them in the dimness.

"Mame'll be at the office," Mr. MacClaren said cryptically, and Mr. Peterson promptly turned the horse's head down a side street, toward the river again. Here the buildings crowded around the muddy road — helter-skelter they stood, often surrounded by great piles of lumber. Rose forgot her fears for a moment and looked around her. There seemed to be no order or plan to what she saw. The buildings were large and small, old and new. Most were constructed of raw wood, either still fresh from the sawmill, or greyed with the rains of years. The buggy stopped before such a building. Mr. MacClaren and Mr. Peterson helped their daughters down, Jakie vaulting to the ground by himself.

Before Rose's feet had touched the ground, her mother was with her, crushing her in a hug, scolding and laughing at once.

"Rose, oh, Rose, what have you been doing? Francis Wilson told us something when he got here early this morning with that . . . that criminal! It can't be true. It can't! Oh, you're so wicked. I'm so glad you're safe!" Rose was somewhat bewildered but she did not have time to answer or question because Mr. Borden came through the door also, with Mrs. Peterson and a tall, stout, gentleman sporting a flowered cravat, tall beaver hat, magnificent sideburns, and a long cigar in his hand.

Mrs. Peterson and Emma clung tightly while Mr. Borden addressed Rose. At first she was frightened and thought he meant to fire her father, or punish her himself, but then she listened closely as Mr. Borden talked and gestured, pointing now and then at the tall gentleman.

". . . the city and all the honest logging companies thank you for all you have done to bring this feller to justice." Rose didn't think he meant the tall man. He must mean the man-catcher. Slowly, she realized he was talking to her, about her. Her eyes widened.

". . . real hero-eyene. . . ."

"And Jakie and Emma, too," put in Rose in a high, tremulous voice.

"Of course, of course. Anyways, we want you kiddies. . . ."

Jake scowled ferociously.

". . . to have a reward of some kind and Mr. Boltworth here'll see that you get it." Mr. Borden stopped with some satisfaction on his face and turned to the tall stranger.

"Haarrrumph," the man began. The rest of his speech was a magnificent ramble of strange, long words and incoherent phrases. Rose, Jakie and Emma took it that he was thanking them.

At last his speech reached a climax and the three could understand him very well.

". . . want you to accept, as souvenirs, these log ends with the genuine brands upon them, which the dastard whom you apprehended chose to sever from their parent log." He reached inside the door of the building and brought out a heavy bundle. It was a pile of three log ends — from fairly small logs — and doled them out, one to each child. The three looked in bewilderment at their presents.

Rose's mother nudged her, as did Mrs. Peterson. Together they stammered, "Th-th-thank you, sir."

"Thank you, sir," muttered Jakie.

"Bless you, my children," said the man and disappeared into the building. Mr. Borden nodded uncomfortably at the little group and followed him in.

The group stood silently for a moment and then, with murmurs, set off up the street with Mr. Peterson in his buggy, Mr. MacClaren following with Jakie, disappearing upstream where he would spend the night with his father in the wanigan.

After a while Rose spoke. "What's it for, Mama?"

"Just a souvenir, Rose." Rose thought her mother sounded a little disgusted and angry.

"Is this the reee-ward, Ma?" asked Emma.

"I reckon," answered Mrs. Peterson.

"I wisht it was a hundred dollars," said Emma softly.

The buggy rattled on through the rain.

17 Pin-whacker

Emma didn't get a licking.

"I think Ma's afraid of Mr. Borden. And that Mr. Boltworth. I guess that souvenir was 'bout as good as a hundred dollars," she confided to Rose.

Even though they weren't spanked, the girls were kept inside for the rest of the day. They helped in the kitchen, they played with the baby, and they swept the floors. By supper time the rain had stopped and piles of pink clouds decorated the sky as the sun fell lower in the west.

"We'll go out tomorrow, Rose."

"What about school, Emma? Don't you have to go?"

"No school during the drive," said Emma with satisfaction, shaking the tablecloth out the back door.

"Why not?"

"Too loud. You'll see tomorrow."

In the morning, Rose understood. The night before, she had gone to bed so quickly, crawling in beside Emma and sinking into her lovely grass-filled mattress, that she went to sleep without noticing the din that filled the streets of the town. Now, insistently, it awakened her. For a while she lay puzzling over the sounds. Finally, she nudged Emma.

"Emma," she whispered and shook the other girl's shoulder, "Emma, what *is* all the noise?"

"Hmmm?" said Emma, opening her eyes part way.

"I said, what's the noise?"

"Oh." And Rose could see that Emma was listening drowsily. "Just . . . noise, I guess. I can hear the sawmills, that sudden squealing; the river with all the logs, that's the booming noise. And there's lotsa loggers in town and they're all shoutin', I guess." She ended her recital with finality and turned over again.

Rose continued to listen. When she could stand it no longer, she wakened Emma again and this time managed to get her out of bed.

"I've just got to see what's going on!" she explained. Emma sighed.

After breakfast they helped Mrs. Peterson and Mrs. MacClaren clean the house and do some baking.

"Nat should be here today, on the wanigan," said Mrs. MacClaren, rolling bread dough from her fingers.

"You'll be glad to see him, I guess," said Mrs. Peterson.

"Yes. I don't think it's the right life for him, but he loves it so and works so hard."

"He's a good boy," said the other woman. Both mothers sighed with satisfaction. Rose and Emma looked at each other thoughtfully.

At last Mrs. Peterson said they could go and the girls

174

ran out into the spring sunshine.

"The best place now is on the rise above the booming grounds!" shouted Emma as she and Rose hurried through the crowded, noisy streets.

Emma's friends were there, too, watching the scene below.

The booming grounds were stretched out before them. Here the drive ended. Part of the river was walled off and Rose for a while couldn't puzzle out how the wall had been built. A word or two spoken by the boys and girls around her gave her the clue. Flat timbers, wide as sidewalks, were chained together, actually walling off the surface of the river on one side: this was the principal boom. The big enclosure made by these timbers — called "boomsticks" — led into a bottleneck. Past the bottleneck were many smaller enclosures. These were the pocket booms, and each owner who had timber in that drive had a pocket boom.

Once the logs reached the main boom, men with pike poles took over the sorting. The river hogs were done now and made their way from the river into the town. "Lookin' fer likker!" shouted one boy behind them. Rose blushed.

At the bottleneck, sorters and checkers stood on the boomsticks calling out the marks on the long ends, making sure each log was pulled into the right pocket boom. This was done by pin-whackers, who listened for the sorters' calls to tell them where each log belonged. The pin-whacker gathered together the logs with the same mark, creating rafts by whacking a pin, or kind of bolt, into a log, running a rope through a hole in the pinhead, whacking a pin into the next log and pulling the rope through that pin, and so on, until he'd built a manageable raft, right there on the river. Logs were easier to move this way, to the mills, to the docks, wherever they were headed.

Rose thought it hardly seemed like a river here. The chained boomsticks might have been an enormous harness for some incredible animal. Only among the pocket booms could she see much water, like places where the scales had dropped from this gigantic lizard. Back up the river, the stream was solid again with long logs, moving in strangely patterned waves, dark and shiny in the sun, like scales moving on a restless beast.

Rose was fascinated, watching the swift, skilled men practice their arts. The pin-whackers interested her most. They were light, agile young men who seemed to enjoy the hectic work. Up and down the boomsticks they ran, across the logs themselves, sometimes teetering precariously like dancers above the bobbing river. She listened to the sorters and checkers call out the marks as they saw them and watched the pin-whacker invariably hook the right log, whirl the log into the right pocket boom, whack in the pin, start a raft or finish one, and send it down the river toward a mill.

One of the pin-whackers seemed less expert than the rest, and though the other boys and girls laughed at his mistakes, his near-misses, Rose sympathized silently and hoped he wouldn't fall, or make too serious a mistake. She watched him for some time before she realized he looked very familiar. She thrust her head forward, excitedly.

"It's Nat!" she squeaked, not even heard above the roaring from the river.

"What?" asked Emma.

"Emma, come, please, come hurry! It's important!"

176

Rose tugged at her friend's sleeve, urging her back from the river, down the small hill away from the booming grounds.

"Emma," she said, when it was quieter, "that was Nat, there in the . . . pocket boom. The poor one, who didn't know what he was doing. He'll be killed! I've gotta get him out of there!"

"Don't be silly, Rose. How could you? They wouldn't let us anywhere near there." Emma's voice was filled with distress. "Find your father. Tell him."

"Let's go!" Rose raced away, followed by Emma.

Through the crowded, muddy streets they ran, toward the office shack where the day before they had been given their rewards. Down the main street they sped, dodging shanty boys and horses. In front of one saloon loggers were lying in an unconscious row, snoring dreadfully. Rose hardly noticed, hurrying by.

A voice called her name. She turned, thinking one of the unconscious loggers had called her. Instead, Jakie appeared at her side, a bundle under his arm.

"Where ya' goin' in such a hurry?"

"Where's my papa, Jakie? Do you know? It's Nat! He's down at the pocket booms. He's down at the pocket booms! He's pin-whacking!" The horror in her voice didn't erase the grin from Jakie's face.

"Is he! By golly, he's a good one, he is! But why do you want your pa?"

"To go get Nat, of course. Our mama didn't want him on the river. And . . . and he might get killed," she finished lamely.

"He ain't much good, Jakie," said Emma, who had joined them.

"Oh, I see. Well, let's try the company office."

And away they ran.

Rose's father was nowhere to be found. She and Emma stood outside the small office. Rose was crying now, tears of frustration and fear. Emma was holding her arm, pulling gently.

"We'll find your ma, Rose, she'll know what to do."

The three ran to Emma's house. The house was silent.

"Where are they? Where, oh where?" cried Rose.

"Gone marketing, I s'pose," said Emma.

They sat down on the front steps, defeated.

After a few minutes, Rose jumped up.

"I've got to do something!" Her voice was high.

"All right, let's go see if we can find your ma. I 'spect I know where they'll be."

"Why didn't you say so?" There was anger in Rose's voice. Emma looked fearful and ran ahead down the street.

At the end of the street, the three began dodging again through the packs of shanty boys who roamed the streets. Suddenly Rose was pulled up short by a giant hand. She looked around fearfully and then broke into a tearful smile.

"Francis Wilson! Oh, maybe you can help!"

The big logger's smile of greeting faded a little, and he asked, "What can I do, Miss Rose?"

"Oh, it's Nat! Somehow he's got a job as a pin-whacker and Mama and Papa don't know about it and he's not very good and I'm scared he'll be killed!"

"Should think so! A pin-whacker, huh! That boy's got guts. 'Scuse the language, ladies. Well, show me where he is. I'll see what I can do."

Rose, infected by her mother's fears, was amazed at the calmness with which Francis Wilson accepted her incredible news. Emma seemed less surprised.

178

They walked toward the rise over the booming-grounds from which Rose had seen her brother. She half wondered if he'd still be there. It seemed as if hours had passed. When they reached the top of the small hill and looked down, the sun still cast the same shadows, the water here and there still glinted and danced, the boys and girls still sat or lay and watched the scene below.

Francis Wilson watched, too, for a minute and then slowly began to make his way down to the river's edge. Rose wondered what he would do, how he would get to Nat. When he reached the river bank, he stopped for a moment or two, looking up and down. Then, calmly and surely, he leaped from the shore onto one of the rafts in a pocket boom, and nimbly, for one so huge, walked smoothly from one to another, reaching the boomsticks at the bottleneck and walking along . . .

"As if he were downtown," said Rose admiringly.

She searched the scene for several minutes before she located Nat, who was struggling near the entrance to the bottleneck with an enormous log.

"There he is!" she said to Emma.

Francis Wilson, too, had seen him and was walking toward him.

"Why doesn't he call to him? Or wave?" asked Rose anxiously.

"I guess he's afraid Nat might fall in if he's startled," replied Emma.

With the noise, the busy, sun-filled river, the danger, her fears were almost too much for Rose. She clapped her hands over her mouth to hold back a small scream.

Calmly crossing the entrances to the pocket booms on logs and rafts, Francis Wilson had almost reached Nat when it happened.

As Nat pulled at his gigantic log, another pin-whacker

179

jauntily approached. The boomstick on which they were working teetered crazily as Nat wrestled with the log. The other pin-whacker was grinning, Rose could see that, even from where she stood. He cupped his hands around his mouth and shouted something at Nat. But his jauntiness was poorly timed; his foot slipped and into the water he fell. Nat evidently heard the splash and turned instantly, still holding the pike pole in his log. Rose could see that he knew right away that the other boy would be caught between the log and the boomstick, and saw him immediately thrust his weight to push at the log. When it began to float slowly away, he let go of the pike pole, leaving it standing at an angle in the log and hurried to where his fellow worker had fallen in. The boy was groping wildly for the boomstick, and Nat kneeled carefully near him and reached for the thrashing arms. He almost fell in himself once or twice, but finally managed to get hold of a handful of the other's shirt and pulled him roughly back toward the plank on which he knelt. Rose could almost hear the boy in the water screaming, but Nat's lips were tightly shut as he hauled and heaved to get the other out of the river.

Finally, the other pin-whacker lay on his stomach across the board, panting hard. Nat rose and looked out toward his log, bobbing majestically beyond reach. His pike pole began to teeter, pulling itself out of the log; then it splashed into the water, and its heavy, iron-sheathed end carried it smoothly down and out of sight. If it came up again, Rose couldn't see it.

Francis Wilson had reached him now, and Rose saw him clap Nat on the shoulder. Then both pointed and gestured at the place the pike pole had disappeared. Now another man joined them, an older man.

180

"He's in charge," said Emma, "now Nat'll get it!"

"Get it!" laughed Rose. "He just saved that boy's life! His *life!*"

"Don't matter," put in Jakie. "The pike pole belongs to the company and that's more important."

Rose was speechless with anger and amazement. She sat down suddenly on the grass and opened and closed her mouth silently a few times.

"You look like a fish, Rose," said Jakie.

"But . . . but."

"That's the way it is," Jakie spoke in a theatrical tone, annoying Rose further. "It's a hard life, you know that. And, listen, you know that log pirate we caught? Well, they came close to stringing him up right there and they would have, 'cept you girls were there."

"Then I'm glad we were," said Rose emphatically.

Jakie gave a sneer, but was silent.

Down on the booming-grounds Nat stood crestfallen between Francis Wilson and the foreman, but at last he and Francis Wilson set off along the boomsticks and toward the shore.

In a little while Francis Wilson and Nat appeared at the top of the hill. Nat looked sullen and bewildered.

"Lost your pike pole and then your job!" shouted one of the boys who had been watching.

"You're no pin-whacker!" jeered another.

Francis Wilson stood among them.

"He done right. Keep that in mind, boys and girls." He said nothing more and the others fell silent.

Nat started to walk toward town. In a second Rose followed, as did Emma. Jakie stayed where he was, intent again on the scene below. Francis Wilson set out after Nat also. He caught up with him and flung an arm around the boy's shoulders.

"C'mon, boy," Rose heard him say, "let's go talk to your pa. He's a good man, he'll understand."

Rose wasn't sure, now, what there was to understand. For a moment, she thought about the cutting, the drive. The log pirate, the fight, the dark Christmas in the bunkhouse flashed through her mind. She shook her head and followed her brother.

Before she had left the small hill entirely, she looked over the town and far down the river, almost to the bay, and saw the wooden houses, the wooden piers, the wooden ships, their tall masts pointing toward the sky.

"All from logging," she muttered, and followed the others.

18 Parting

The drive was almost over. The last Duck Tree logs were in the pocket booms, the piles of sawdust at the mills had started to grow, the whirr and squeal of the saws sounded all day long. Rose and her friends watched ships tie up at the wharves, sails furled, or engines turned off, while they were loaded with lumber for Chicago or Buffalo. Once in a while the logs went lashed together as rafts: a tug or schooner would pull long lines of them down the lakes.

One day Rose and her mother packed their things and started back to Duck Tree Camp. Emma cried noisily as the wagon started down the muddy street. Rose let a few tears come into her eyes too.

She remembered how it had been the fall before, when she and her mother had driven the same road. How romantic and exciting Duck Tree Camp had seemed then, as she looked forward to a winter there.

For a while they traveled near the river. It was almost empty now, as it had been then. Here and there a log bobbed gently near the banks, caught by an invisible sandbar, or the projecting root of a tangled osier. In one place, where a small stream entered the main branch, a dozen or more logs had gathered and gotten caught in an eddy against the downstream side of the little creek. Rose thought of the log pirate and shivered. Two men from the boom company were working there, shouting curses at one another as they freed the logs and prepared to raft them down toward town.

The river bank was scarred and raw, strewn with bark and muddled by scores of caulked boots.

Mrs. MacClaren guided Snowball away from the river, across country, in a shorter, more direct route to camp. The endless aisles of pines Rose remembered from her first trip were gone. The newly cut-over land was raw and barren. Stumps seemed to stretch for miles, and here and there the remains of tote roads and skidways left curious patterns. Piles of slashings filled little hollows and rose against the sky. As far as she could see it looked like this, the dreariness broken here and there by a lonely stand of birch or maple, now and then a beech, which hadn't been in the way of the loggers.

Soon they reached the empty acres through which they had passed in October. Compared with the newly cut-over land, these gentle slopes seemed almost lush to Rose. Second-growth pines poked above the thin, bright green grass that covered the dull black-brown of the burned-over land. Here and there, nervous, fluttering aspen seedlings flourished and waved their budding twiglets above the rest.

"Aren't there any wild animals?" asked Rose idly.

184

"There are some, of course, Rose, but very few around the places that are being logged. Especially not little animals." She flapped the reins over Snowball's back, but the horse only swiveled her eyes once and continued at a comfortable walk. "There used to be beavers, of course, and martens, but the trappers killed them off a long time ago. And the otters. And the muskrats." She paused for a moment, thinking "There used to be lots of fish, too, but there aren't so many now."

"The trapping is bad enough," she went on, "but it's the burning, too. All the little animals disappear. And the rivers are choked with mud."

"Why do they do it? Burn it over, I mean."

"Well, it clears the slashings and all the trash and stumps. It's supposed to make it better farmland, too."

"Does it?"

"Your papa says not, but some say it does."

They were silent for a few minutes and then Rose said, "Well, it all seems like a terrible waste! The animals, the trees, the land, all of it."

"No. We need the lumber," her mother answered with firm lips. "For houses and railroad ties, and fence posts, of course, and to burn. And for ships."

Parades of wooden buildings, ships, and miles of train tracks flashed through Rose's mind. She felt torn between these things. The small animals cried piteously in her head, but so did the babies living in wooden houses.

Just then two crows called from among the stumps. Their voices seemed filled with desolate anger. They wheeled above and landed and rose again into the air among the ruin of their ancient resting site.

"There were crows at Grandpa's."

185

"I know."

"He said they'd been coming to the same spot since long before the settlers first came." She thought of her grandmother's house, square and white, with half-moons cut into the green shutters. She thought probably the wood had come from just such a forest as this had been. She sighed.

"Don't try to solve it, dear."

Snowball ambled onward.

They reached Duck Tree Camp, and Rose was hardly prepared for the silence and deserted air, although she knew the shanty boys had left some days before. They were all gone now, some to their farms and families, most of them to handle lumber again, this time on the ships that carried it away. She hadn't realized how much the people had meant to the life of the camp.

The doors to the bunkhouse were closed, and already a spider web glimmered across the latch. The blacksmith shop was closed and seemed smaller than Rose remembered. The cookhouse was still open and near the kitchen door stood the O'Connors' wagon and the two brown horses that pulled it. They were going back to their farm too, where Mrs. O'Connor would cook all the meals, Rose supposed, while Jakie and his father farmed.

Their own cabin seemed less deserted. The chickens still trilled and clucked and gargled in their pen at one

end. Rose would shortly put them in a coop for traveling home. But not yet. The MacClarens had packed nothing before they left for town in such a hurry and now it was all to be done. It was now the middle of the afternoon, and Rose and her mother worked until sunset, packing, sweeping, cleaning and carrying things to the wagon.

Before supper, Mrs. MacClaren handed Rose the milk pail, and her daughter wandered slowly across the clearing, looking at the rosy sky that turned the cut-over land beyond the camp into a pink-tinged sea.

She met her father coming from the van.

"I'll milk, Rosy," he said, taking the pail from her and going ahead into the barn. She stood behind him while the warm milk banged into the pail.

"Where's Francis Wilson, Papa?"

"Gone, Rose. On his way."

"But where to? Does he have a wife and children and farm, too?"

"No, Rose. He's a drifter, I guess you'd say."

"But where's he gone to?"

"Well, I guess he's gone to Oregon. He likes to travel."

"Oregon! But that's so far away. Will he be back?"

"Hard to say. I 'spect so. He likes Michigan and usually comes back for the winter cutting."

"Will we be back, Papa?"

"What a lot of questions, Rose." He sounded weary and leaned his forehead against the cow.

"Will we?"

"I don't know. I like the life myself. . . ."

"You do?" she interrupted, surprised.

"Yes. I do. It's hard, but I've got a good berth, as scaler. People always need timber and lumber and, well, the farming here is bad, and lonesome and uncertain. There's nothing else like it, the logging, I mean. It's as good as whaling, when you think about it. Outdoors, struggling with giant things, with men who aren't putting on a show of any kind. . . ." Rose thought he wasn't talking to her now. "Doing something *important!*" The milk stopped in a dribble and he stopped talking. He rose from the milking stool.

"But Mama doesn't like it, does she?"

"No, not particularly." He handed Rose the pail.

"Why?"

"Better ask her." He started back toward the van. "Tell her I'll be over for supper shortly."

Rose started toward the cabin. The O'Connors' wagon was still drawn up back of the cookhouse. Jakie came through the door and, seeing Rose, waved wildly.

She paused, and rested the pail on the ground. Jakie pelted to her side.

" 'Lo, Rose. When ya goin'?"

"Tomorrow, I guess."

"So're we! Thought we'd be leavin' today, but the baby was poorly, so we're stayin'."

"I hope he's better soon."

"Who? Oh, the baby. Yeah, I guess he will be. Where you off to?"

"Oh, just home. The farm. I've never been there."

"Yeah, us, too. But it'll take us three days to get there!"

"So far!"

"Yep. Down in Indiana."

"I didn't know!" Rose realized how little she knew about Jakie. Or Francis Wilson, or Army, or Jack, or any of the rest.

"Jakie, don't the men ever talk about their homes?"

"Naw, why should they? You see, lots of 'em come 'cause they don't like where they live, or what they did before or . . . or . . . other things," he finished lamely.

"I see." She was going to say more, but thought better of it, and reached down to pick up her pail. The pink in the sky was purple now, rapidly turning to gray. The miles of stumps looked ugly again.

"Well, good-bye, Jakie. Will you be here next year?"

"Who knows? My pa's talking about going out west. To Indian territory."

"Oh, Jakie!"

"Yep. Well, 'by' Rose. Let me know if you ever want to catch any log pirates again." He laughed and ran back toward the cookhouse.

" 'Bye." She waved after his back.

The family was all together at supper.

"It's been so long," commented Mrs. MacClaren, with a smile.

"Wisht *I* was on my way to Oregon with Francis Wilson," said Nat.

"Nat . . . !" said his mother.

"Need you on the farm this summer, son," said Mr. MacClaren.

"I know, Pa, I know. I ain't goin' no place."

"Nat!" said his mother severely. "Please watch the way you speak. Those shanty boys . . . ," she finished, muttering.

"Yes, Ma." He pushed away his plate and leaned back from the table. "Well, Rose. How'd you like it? Loggin', I mean."

"Hmmm. Well, I enjoyed it lots. But it wasn't quite what I thought, I guess. I thought it would be all exciting and there'd be lots to watch and so on, and it

190

was that way, partly. But partly it was, oh, wild, and not pleasant, and hard, I guess."

"Yes, I know what you mean, Rose," said Mrs. Mac-Claren. "It seems as if it should be romantic and adventurous, but mostly it's plain hard, grueling work."

"But satisfying, Mame."

"Hmmm." Mrs. MacClaren rose and began clearing the table.

"And it looks so awful where it's been cut over," added Rose.

"Oh, it'll come back," Nat and his father said together.

"You'll see," went on Nat, "and there are blueberries, lots and lots of 'em where it's been cut and burned."

Rose's face brightened.

"I'll show you where, when we get to the farm tomorrow."

The next day went quickly in a jumble of packing and traveling. The wagon, followed by Nat and the cow, went slowly across country and down overgrown tracks for hours, until it reached the MacClarens' homestead. Then there was the jumble of unpacking, of arranging the kitchen, settling the cow, exploring the barn and the house.

Finally, Rose was alone in the small room that would

be hers. The sun was setting again. Long, streaming white clouds pointed out the orange sun shining warmly through her window. She was taking things from her carpetbag, hanging dresses on hooks behind the door, putting her nightgowns and her petticoats in the drawers of her small dresser. The bag was almost empty now. She reached in one more time and, with a puzzled expression on her face, lifted, with both hands, a heavy object at the bottom. When she had it out, she laughed and held the object up.

It was the "ree-ward" that Mr. Boltworth had given her. She looked around the room and then turned to the dresser and propped the awkward piece of wood beside her small mirror. The sun's rich rays turned the surface of the raw wood to a golden yellow. And in relief, the shadows deepening it, was the Duck Tree symbol.

"Well, I'll never forget, I guess," she sighed, smiling.

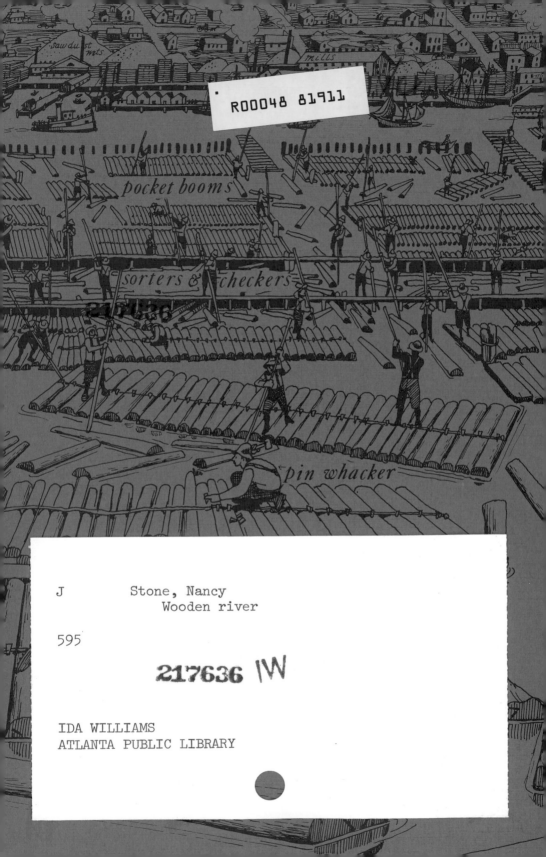